Confirming
the Faith
of Adolescents

An Alternative Future for Confirmation

Edited by Arthur J. Kubick

PAULIST PRESS
New York/Mahwah

Library of Congress Cataloging-in-Publication Data

Confirming the faith of adolescents: an alternative future for confirmation/ edited by Arthur J. Kubick.
    p.   cm.
  Includes bibliographical references.
  ISBN 0-8091-3236-2
  1. Confirmation.   I. Kubick, Arthur J., 1939–   .
BV815.C64   1991
234′.162—dc20   90-29008
                                                                                    CIP

Published by Paulist Press
997 Macarthur Boulevard
Mahwah, New Jersey 07430

Printed and bound in the United States of America

CONTENTS

III. *Confirming Adolescents: Alternatives*

INTRODUCTION

Arthur J. Kubick

The years since Vatican II have brought an explosion of exciting new insights into the meaning of Christian life in society. Our common call to be both citizens and disciples, rooted as it is in our biblical stories, has sounded even more clearly in recent years—deepened and clarified by brothers and sisters in the third world, and by the dogged witness of Dorothy Day, Thomas Merton, Martin Luther King, Desmund Tutu and so many others. Perhaps the key word for the 1970s and 1980s has been "ministry," a growing awareness among church members that all are called to service in church and world. In his *Theology of Ministry* Thomas O'Meara speaks of this ministry flowing from baptism. It is public activity using charisms of the Spirit present in each personality to help realize the reign of God in a local community. The movement is always outward, beyond a church-centered mentality, toward the realization of God's reign in society.

This vision has particularly touched our understanding and celebration of sacraments. John Shea's capsulized summary of eucharist points to this: "Gather the folks/Tell the stories/Break the bread." And from this celebration move to the day-to-day work in society. Celebrating sacraments does not dead-end in ecclesial navel-gazing; rather it impels the community to renewed energy for the reign of God. Latin American theologians have continually reminded us of this vision, rooted as it is in the Bible and in a way of doing theology which begins with attentiveness to God's Spirit moving within the experience of people. Sacramental theology begins here, they remind us, through involvement in the struggle for human freedom and dignity; not in isolated reflection on texts and ideas separated from daily life.

The renewal of the sacraments of initiation flowing from

1

Vatican II—the Rite of Baptism for Children (1969), the Rite of Confirmation (1971) and the Rite of Christian Initiation of Adults (1972)—has brought a life-giving energy to our celebration of these rites. Thanks to the persistent work of groups such as the North American Forum on the Catechumenate the RCIA has become a vibrant reality in parishes throughout the United States. But this renewal has also raised questions about initiation practice, centered specifically on what has become common practice in most dioceses across the country: infant baptism, first eucharist around age seven, and confirmation during adolescence (in most cases around age sixteen). For a number of years now the initiation debate/dialogue has considered the theological, liturgical, pastoral and developmental issues surrounding the initiation sacraments. The crux of this debate has been confirmation, a sacrament which some see as floundering without a theology, and others consider a life-giving movement of the Spirit. A brief look at the parameters of the debate may help toward clarifying the issues.

Two especially helpful deliniations of the discussion have come from John Roberto and Mark Searle. In his 1978 resource paper, "Confirmation in the American Catholic Church," written for the National Conference of Diocesan Directors (NCDD), John Roberto classified current approaches to confirmation into the "liturgical-initiation" school and the "theological-maturity" school. He describes the "liturgical-initiation" school as approaching confirmation "as an integral element of the entire initiatory process within an ecclesial community."[1] It receives its impetus from the revised Rite of Confirmation and the RCIA. In contrast the "theological-maturity" school views confirmation as "the rite of passage into Christian adulthood, the celebration of Christian maturity, the sacrament of witness and Christian mission, the time for decision, choice and commitment, the sacrament of Christian adulthood, the strengthening of the Spirit for mission, the communication of the grace of Pentecost and the conferral of the full rights of membership in the faith community."[2]

Mark Searle takes the discussion a step further by suggesting three different models flowing from an historical perspective: the patristic model, the Roman model, and the reformation model.[3]

The patristic model, or the "unitary-sacramental" tradition, corresponds to Roberto's "liturgical-initiation" school. The practice during the early Christian centuries was to celebrate the unity of the paschal mystery in a cluster of rites, usually during the Easter vigil. Baptism-confirmation-eucharist came together in one celebration, with "confirmation" seen as sealing the baptism and preparing the person for full sharing in the eucharist.

The Roman model, so named because of the influence of the Roman church, began to develop as early as the third century, but became the norm during the middle ages. Searle calls it the "confirmation-as-an-independent-sacrament" tradition because it sets confirmation as a sacrament apart from baptism, speaking of it in terms of strengthening and witness.

Finally, the reformation model, dating from the sixteenth century, sees confirmation primarily from the perspective of personal faith. This is the "confirmation-as-affirmation-of-faith" tradition, which has strongly influenced Roman Catholic practice, particularly the catechetical structure of preparation for confirmation.

To oversimplify, the current dialogue/debate centers around two understandings of confirmation. One, grounded in the patristic model, maintains that the Vatican II initiation reforms call for the restored sequence of the initiation sacraments: baptism, confirmation, eucharist—a unitary-sacramental view. Confirmation seals baptism and leads to eucharist. This vision rooted in the paschal mystery has been summed up in #215 of the RCIA, insisting that adults (and children of catechetical age) "are not to be baptized without receiving confirmation immediately afterwards, unless some serious reason stands in the way." Mark Searle, Aidan Kavanaugh, Gerard Austin and most liturgists have been strong proponents of this view, seeing the common practice of celebrating confirmation in adolescence, many years after first eucharist, as an aberration. While the baptism-confirmation-eucharist order is now the norm throughout the United States for adult catechumens and for children of catechetical age (cf. the

RCIA), some parishes and dioceses are also experimenting with confirmation celebrated with first eucharist. The Sacramento, California diocese, for example, has been piloting such a process in conjunction with the development of "belonging rites" for adolescents.

On the other hand, especially since Vatican II (and, many would say, as a direct result of its vision), confirmation as an independent sacrament celebrated with adolescents has become the norm in most dioceses. Since 1970 the age for confirmation has steadily risen into the sophomore, junior and even senior years of high school. Along with this has come a deepening awareness of confirmation in relation to the other initiation sacraments, an awareness hightened by the RCIA. The majority of U.S. bishops, even while acknowledging certain theological inconsistencies, support adolescent confirmation as the most pastorally sound direction for our society. Those who see confirmation as an independent sacrament—intimately related to baptism and eucharist—stress that it is:

- an initiation sacrament;
- the end of a long catechumenal process bracketed by infant baptism and confirmation;
- a sacrament that commissions a person for carrying out the mission of the public church;
- an opening for youth and adults to the leadings of the Spirit;
- a remembering and reactivating of the fundamental sacrament of baptism within the church community.

This pastoral concern which is at the core of their position flows from a central principle: sacraments are for people, not people for sacraments. Hence the need to move even beyond the argument between the liturgists and the pastoralists—an argument which reminds one of the struggle in the early church between Gentiles and Jews. The real issue is what will happen to the people being confirmed and to society, not what will happen to the church. Thomas Marsh, Gérard Fourez, Kieran Sawyer, and Henri Bourgeois have been the main proponents of this independent sacrament tradition. Joining them have been a large number of youth ministers, directors of religious education and, as mentioned above, diocesan bishops. Some would even argue that the sensus fidelium rests on this pastoral side of the issue.[4]

Often the two positions in this dialogue/debate seem irreconcilable. In fact there are times when one side appears to shut off discussion, considering the matter closed thanks to canon law, the RCIA, and historical research. This "Roma locuta, cause finita est" position leads only to deeper divisions between the two positions. What is needed is a respectful listening to one another coupled with a thoughtful challenging of one another's treasured assumptions. Only in such an atmosphere of honest discussion can a true pastoral direction emerge, a direction rooted in the experience of people and attentive to the reign of God breaking forth in our world.

This book hopes to enter into the discussion by offering one side of the confirmation dialogue/debate as clearly as possible. The legitimate concerns and experiences of those who have worked with adolescent confirmation may contribute toward a renewed understanding of this often misunderstood sacrament. These essays are presented with an openness to further dialogue. Hopefully they will be received by readers in the same spirit. Together we may all find ourselves listening to the one Spirit who calls us all to follow, often leading in directions we ordinarily would not go.

The Essays in This Book

Part I of this book, "Confirming Adolescents: The Theory," considers the bases for our present baptism-eucharist-confirmation practice with serious looks at scripture, theology, church documents and current practice. Thomas Marsh, Kieran Sawyer, Gérard Fourez and Richard Reichert offer unique perspectives on the question, arguing for the celebration of confirmation with adolescents on both theological and pastoral grounds. According to Thomas Marsh initiation practices in Acts clearly reveal two rites. Arguing from an historical perspective he shows that Christian initiation is primarily concerned with producing a mature member of the church able to personally appropriate the gift of faith. Kieran Sawyer finds this same insistence in contemporary theologies and conciliar documents. This leads her to present a carefully considered case for celebrating confirmation with adolescents. In his article, "Toward a Pastoral Theology of Confirmation," Gérard Fourez argues that young people should not have to prove themselves worthy of the sacrament because confirmation chiefly celebrates the coming of the Spirit into the Christian community. His essay might best be read in conjunction with that of Theresa Viramontes-Gutierrez in Part II as a pastoral application of his reflections. Richard Reichert's essay rounds out this section with a consideration of the paschal mystery as the paradigm for all of revelation; hence the sacrament of confirmation must be understood in relationship to it.

The essays of Arthur Kubick, Lynn Neu and Theresa Viramontes-Gutierrez bring this discussion into the practical day-to-day sphere in Part II, "Confirming Adolescents: Current and Future Practice." Their own broad pastoral experience makes their insights into this question especially valuable. Arthur Kubick's essay focuses on one parish's experience celebrating confirmation with adolescents, a preparation influenced by the vision of the RCIA. In "Confirmation at Age Sixteen: Milwaukee's Story," Lynn Neu offers us a portrait of confirmation practice in the archdiocese of Milwaukee and looks at various diocesan policies throughout the United States. Preparing for confirmation is a journey in faith calling all involved to integrate their human experience with the Christian experience. Theresa Viramontes-Gutierrez shows how this approach to confirmation preparation identifies and responds well to the specific needs and concerns of Hispanic youth and their families.

Ecumenical concerns and a search for alternative futures for confirmation are necessary ingredients of any dialogue about this sacrament. Therefore Part III, "Confirming Adolescents: Alternatives," includes essays from Gary Davis, a UCC minister, John Westerhoff of Duke University, and Craig Cox, a canon lawyer/theologian from the Los Angeles archdiocese. Each of them takes us a bit further beyond our comfortable horizons to consider other possibilities, new configurations for confirmation. Rev.

Gary Davis gives us a careful history of initiation, noting how the reformers understood this in the sixteenth century, and then offers a Protestant perspective on our present theology of confirmation. In recent years the Episcopal Church has reformed its initiation practices. John Westerhoff surveys this reform and challenges the practice of adolescent confirmation, offering in its place two rites—one at the beginning of adolescence and another around age eighteen to mark the transition to adulthood. (Readers interested in the initiation reforms in the Lutheran, Presbyterian, United Methodist and Episcopal Churches might also read Gerard Austin's chapters on this in his book, *Anointing with the Spirit,* New York: Pueblo Publishing Co., 1985.) Finally, in his essay, "Rethinking Confirmation," Graig Cox proposes a solution to the confirmation dialogue/debate. His suggestion that we consider "repeatable confirmation," celebrating the sacrament at significant moments throughout the life cycle, deserves serious consideration by liturgists, sacramental theologians and all concerned about the future of the church community as a living presence within society. It impels us to imagine, to—in the words of Robert Kennedy—"dream things that never were and ask why not."

In conclusion, Bernard Cooke offers his reflections on the sacrament of confirmation, particularly as they accord with the ideas presented in the articles in this book.

Speaking of many nineteen and twenty year olds he meets in his work as a university professor, Michael Warren suggests that every diocese set up new tribunals to deal with "confirmation annulments," freeing these young people from what they consider a ritual they were forced through—and hence who have never really received the sacrament. Of course, many of them might also say that about their baptisms. But he speaks to an important need—the need to clarify our understanding of this initiation sacrament. "Confirmation as the sacrament of the community's commitment to be faithful to the Spirit present in its midst and to hand on that Spirit to all its members needs much more reflection than it has received so far."[5] Hopefully this book will offer a small portion of that necessary reflection.

Perhaps the key words for this book are "gift," "community" and "society." Speaking at the 1990 National Convocation on the Sacrament of Confirmation in Denver, Colorado, Gérard Fourez offered these as central to a proper understanding of confirmation.

> First, I try to say that the sacrament of confirmation should not try to celebrate the commitment of people to be mature people or mature Christians. It is the gift of God, the gracious loving gift of God. To put it otherwise, confirmation, like every Christian sacrament is never a celebration that should be moralizing or telling people what should be done. Confirmation is called to be a celebration, like every sacrament, of the unconditional love and gift from God to our society, not only to the church.
>
> And second, I would say that the sacrament of confirmation is not a celebration that concerns only the person who is called to be confirmed. Actually it concerns all the members of the community and the community as a whole. It is not a celebration for an individual but a celebration of the church, that is, of the whole Christian community when that community discovers that the Spirit speaks in new ways through new members. Then it could be that the celebration of the sacrament of confirmation would take on new meanings in our society. I did not say in our church; I said in our society. Because what is important is that in the end the way we accept the Spirit will make a difference for the suffering in our world —for those who are oppressed, for those who do not have a voice. That is always the test and the criterion: if we worship not in Jerusalem, not in Gerizim, but in truth and love.

This book seeks to speak to and with the community in that same spirit.

NOTES

1. John Roberto, "Confirmation in the American Catholic Church," *The Living Light* 15 (Summer 1978) 267.

2. Ibid. 266.

3. Mark Searle, "Confirmation: The State of the Question," *Church* (Winter 1985) 15–22.

4. See, for example, the article by Edward Jeremy Miller, "Confirmation as Ecclesial Commissioning," *Louvain Studies* 10 (Fall 1984) 106–121.

5. Michael Warren, *Faith, Culture and the Worshipping Community,* New York: Paulist Press, 59.

I

Confirming Adolescents: The Theory

Chapter 1

CHRISTIAN INITIATION:
PRACTICE AND THEOLOGY

Thomas Marsh

The "Problem" of Confirmation

It is only in this century that confirmation has become a significant topic of theological discussion. In previous ages there have indeed been important contributions, most notably that of St. Thomas Aquinas. When in 1439 the Council of Florence issued its ecumenical Decree for the Armenians, it simply summarized and reproduced Aquinas' understanding of this sacrament. Because of its subsequent influence, the text of the Decree on Confirmation merits quotation.

> The effect of this sacrament is that in it the Holy Spirit is given for strength, as he was given to the apostles on the day of Pentecost, in order that the Christian may courageously confess the name of Christ. And, therefore, the one to be confirmed is anointed on the forehead which is the seat of shame, so that he may not be ashamed to confess the name of Christ, and chiefly his cross, which, according to the apostle, is a stumbling block for the Jews and foolishness for the Gentiles. This is why he is signed with the cross.

The understanding of confirmation as a giving of the Holy Spirit to strengthen the recipient to courageously confess the name of Christ subsequently became standard teaching in Catholic theology. The Council of Trent formally defined that confirmation was "a true and proper sacrament," one of the seven "sacraments of the new law." But the meaning of the sacrament was usually presented in terms of the Thomistic understanding and the De-

13

cree for the Armenians. In our times this perspective is often summed up in the description of confirmation as the sacrament of Christian witness and commitment. This is the concept one finds presented by Vatican II (*Lumen Gentium* 11) and the Instruction on the New Rite of Confirmation (1973).

Meanwhile, however, little attention was paid to the history of this sacrament, of either its rite or its theology. In fact, it has only been in this century that many of the documents essential to this task have become available. But while study of this material has greatly enhanced knowledge of the history of confirmation, it has also created new problems. It showed that over wide areas of the church, and particularly in the east, a confirmational rite clearly distinct from baptism did not for certain periods exist. When to this is added the denial or serious questioning of the existence of a rite of confirmation in the New Testament by some scholars, it is easy to see why confirmation is so often described today as constituting "a problem." The sacrament has to face radical and serious questions concerning its origin, history, and theological meaning. This latter concerns basically the relation of confirmation to baptism. If baptism produces all the effects which Christian tradition over the centuries consistently asserts, what additional grace or effect can confirmation possibly add, especially if one sees confirmation (correctly) as a sacrament of initiation? This question has indeed proved a veritable theological conundrum.

The recent discussion concerning confirmation was occasioned by the issuing of the new rites for Christian initiation: Baptism of Children (1969), Confirmation (1971), RCIA (1972). What quickly attracted attention here, however, was not really anything in the rite of confirmation itself, but the flexibility which the accompanying legislation allowed on the age for this sacrament in the case of one baptized as an infant. While reaffirming the existing canonical position that such children be confirmed "about the seventh year," it qualified this by adding that "for pastoral reasons . . . episcopal conferences may choose an age which seems more appropriate so that the sacrament is given at a more mature age after appropriate formation" (Introduction 11).

Though the permission here granted was largely simply recognizing existing practice, since confirmation was usually conferred around the years ten to twelve, many now began to advocate and practice a still later age—mid-teenage, or even later still. Meanwhile the reintroduction of the unified rite of initiation in the RCIA has led others to advocate adhering as closely as possible to this pattern. The question of the appropriate age for confirmation, in the context of infant baptism, has thus led to lively debate and the advocacy and practice of many different options. Directly or indirectly, it forms the context in which the whole question of confirmation is today most often discussed.

Clearly, many considerations enter into and influence a decision on this question. Practical and pastoral factors must be given due weight—and these may vary from place to place. But basically the decision must be taken in the light of the meaning of confirmation as a sacrament of Christian initiation. This meaning, however, can only be established from a study of the history of the sacrament and a critical assessment of the theological understanding which accompanied that history. If one can form an understanding of confirmation from these sources, one may then proceed to apply this to determine the appropriate context for the sacrament in our circumstances today. This is the task which this essay attempts to undertake. Inevitably, however, it can only be a study in outline.

Origins of Christian Initiation

The meaning of a sacramental rite is determined by its origin. What it meant then, it means now. One therefore turns to the New Testament to see how the rite was practiced and understood in the early church. But when one consults the New Testament seeking this information concerning confirmation, one is confronted with a basic problem. There would seem to be very little explicit reference to what, since the fifth century, we now call confirmation in these documents. One can point to two passages in the Acts of the Apostles (8:14–19; 19:1–7) and an oblique reference in Hebrews 6:2, but the confirmational value of even these, the most obvious references, has been disputed. There is therefore at least a large absence of explicit reference to confirmation in the New Testament. Much has been made of this apparent and alleged silence by many scholars. The argument has centered in particular on the silence of St. Paul concerning a post-baptismal initiation rite in contrast with the apparent references of St. Luke in Acts. There has been a tendency to accept St. Paul's silence on this issue as indicating that no such rite existed in his time. Such an attitude gives here a controlling priority to the silence of Paul over against the evidence of Acts, which then has to be explained in some other way.

This whole question is a complicated one. The argument from silence is the most difficult of all arguments in historiography, and the one most open to subjective inclination. The issue can only be treated very summarily here. Two points are important. While scholarly opinion tended to adopt a very skeptical attitude toward the historical value of Acts, the argument could be presented with a certain plausibility. In more recent decades, however, this attitude has changed. There is today a far higher regard for this historical value of St. Luke's document, at least as regards the general character and thought of early Christianity, if not for specific details. This significantly changes the picture. Further, the old argument paid too little attention to the different character and purpose of Paul's writings from that of Luke's, a serious methodological fault. These together with other considerations render the argument from St. Paul's silence too simplistic and ultimately unacceptable. Another approach has to be adopted.

I will assume here, since detailed discussion is not possible, the general historicity of St. Luke's account of early Christianity. When, then, we examine Acts for information on the initiation practice of the early church, we find that the process was a sacramental one consisting of two rites: baptism in the name of Jesus Christ for the forgiveness of sins (2:38; 22:16) and imposition of hands for the gift of the Holy Spirit. Many modern commentators have professed finding this practice of *two* initiation rites incoherent. But once one pays attention to the biblical and Jewish background of Christian initiation, this is not so. Christian faith proclaimed that God's promise to Israel had been fulfilled in Jesus Christ. The prophets had portrayed this fulfillment in terms of the blessings it would involve and realize, the messianic blessings. Ezekiel 36:24–28 is perhaps the classic statement of this perspective. The prophet here describes these blessings as involving three elements and stages: a cleansing of the people from the defilement of sin; renewal of heart (i.e. the moral and religious renewal of the people); finally, as a crowning, sealing effect, the gift of the Spirit of God.

In Judaism the first two of these stages, the cleansing and renewal, would have been seen as one, as simply referring to the negative and positive aspects of the one event. But the gift of the Spirit was a distinct and final event following on this renewal and rendering it secure. This understanding of the messianic blessings now matched the experience on the part of the first, original Christians of the salvation events accomplished in and through Jesus Christ. The blessing of forgiveness of sins/renewal of heart was achieved by Christ through the paschal mystery of his life, death and resurrection. This was the achievement of Easter Sunday, and it could be received through faith in Christ and personal discipleship of him. But Easter Sunday was followed and bore final fruit with the coming of the Holy Spirit on Pentecost. These two events, Easter and Pentecost, the event of Christ and the event of the Spirit, achieved and realized the messianic salvation and brought into existence the messianic community, the Spirit-filled community of the disciples of Christ. This was the community which now possessed and enjoyed the messianic blessings. Others who would receive and share in these blessings could do so by joining this community and becoming members of it. This is the origin and context of the initiation practice of the early church, the origin and context which determined its shape and character.

This initiation process faithfully reflects this background of experience and understanding. New converts joining the community undergo in sacrament the same experience as the original disciples of the events of Easter and Pentecost, the events of Christ and the Spirit. The process therefore involves two rites, one christological, the other pneumatological: baptism in the name of Jesus Christ for the forgiveness of sins and imposition of hands for reception of the Spirit. The rites express the origin and essential character of the community the converts are entering.

When seen from the standpoint of early Christianity, this initiation process is totally coherent. St. Luke's description of this system in Acts has to be accepted as historically accurate.

When one turns now to the writings of St. Paul one finds he is engaged on a different enterprise to that of Luke. He is not interested in narrating or describing the initiation practice of the church. He can and does take this for granted. His interest lies in developing a more profound understanding of this practice. In contrast to Luke, his purpose is explicitly theological. He wishes to stress and express the *unity* which underlies the two rites of initiation, not to distinguish and contrast them with one another. He therefore emphasizes that union with Christ in baptism, being "in Christ," also means sharing in the Spirit of Christ. The two sacramental events express the one reality. But this does not mean he is denying or changing the initiation practice of the church. He is simply approaching the question with a different purpose and different interests to those of Luke. Once this is recognized, there is no basic contradiction between these writers on this issue.

History and Theology

Once it is recognized that Christian initiation in the New Testament period consisted of two rites, baptism for the forgiveness of sins and imposition of hands for the gift of the Holy Spirit, then the subsequent though complicated history of initiation becomes easy to understand and follow. This is certainly true of the western church, to which comment here will be mainly confined. In at least large areas of the eastern church, especially for much of the third and fourth centuries, a different development occurred. But here sufficient documentary evidence is tantalizingly lacking and the whole question, for the moment at least, remains very speculative.

But for the west, at least from the end of the second century on, the evidence is basically clear and reasonably continuous, even if many points of detail remain obscure. Christian initiation here consisted basically and centrally of the two rites mentioned by St. Luke in Acts. Certain developments did however occur and were important for the future. In the course of the second century rites of anointing with oil were added to the baptismal ceremony, both before and after the immersion. In Rome, from at least the early third century, part of the post-baptismal anointing, the chrismation of the forehead, was kept to the end of the whole initiation ceremony and performed by the bishop. Placed in this position, this relatively minor rite became not merely the last and dismissal ceremony of the whole initiation ritual but also came to be associated with the confirmational imposition of hand. Here it came to be the application to each individual candidate of the general imposition of hand over all and its accompanying prayer for the gift of the Spirit. Gradually over the centuries this Roman ritual spread throughout the west, and in our present rite this chrismation is declared to be the essential rite of the sacrament.

Another major and significant development occurred around the beginning of the fifth century. This was the separation of baptism and confirmation into separate ceremonies with a greater or lesser time interval between them. This was a major break with the older tradition of the unified ceremony of initiation at the Easter vigil. But it was a development which the western church felt forced upon it by the great increase in Christian numbers over the fourth century. Converts outside the reach of the episcopal church had to be cared for. In origin the separation of the sacraments was in fact an effort to maintain their unity by retaining the personal ministry of the bishop for the concluding rite of confirmation. The admirable theory was that those baptized in the outlying churches would receive the concluding rite as soon as possible either in the cathedral church itself or when the bishop visited their area. This effort only too quickly proved a vain hope. Over the centuries the interval between baptism and what must often have been the problematic confirmation lengthened into years. Faced with this same situation the Greek church adopted a different solution, allowing the priest to confirm immediately after baptism.

The separation of the two sacraments had an important consequence for the understanding or theology of confirmation. It led to an effort, understandable in the circumstances, to give a meaning to this sacrament as separate from and over against baptism. Eventually confirmation came to be seen not so much as a sacrament of initiation but as concerned with a later state of life. It was seen as conferring a gift of strengthening for the public profession of the faith, a sacrament of witness as it is often termed today. St. Augustine's suggestion of two gifts of the Spirit in Christian initiation, one in baptism and a further in confirmation, here proved a useful formula. Theology thus came to teach that there was a gift of the Spirit in baptism as a principle of sanctification, the Indwelling of the Holy Spirit, and another later in confirmation which strengthened one for the public profession and witness of the faith.

This neat solution has to be regarded as unsatisfactory. We can see from the New Testament that confirmation is a sacrament of initiation intimately linked with baptism. Here these two rites together constitute a complex sacramental process whereby one becomes a member of the church, the Spirit-filled community of Christ. The special reference of confirmation concerns the role of the Holy Spirit in this event. It signifies coming to share in the Spirit of God which fills and animates this community. This is what receiving the Spirit, the gift of the Spirit, means. But the New Testament only recognizes *one* gift of the Spirit, however many aspects it may see in that one gift. It does not parcel out reception of the Spirit into two events. This understanding has implications for our theology and practice of initiation and confirmation today. The idea of two gifts of the Spirit in initiation is too neat a solution and has to be regarded as an unsatisfactory theology.

Confirmation Today

Membership of the church means essentially the mature member, the person capable of professing mature faith. Yet the church insists that the baptized infant is a member of the church.

Any apparent discrepancy between these two statements is resolved by recognizing that the baptized infant is involved in a process of growing and developing toward mature membership, a process which will take years. The implication of this is that the infant, having been incorporated into the Spirit-filled community in baptism, has in fact received the Spirit. But it has received the Spirit as an infant and in accordance with the capacity of an infant. It is beginning a process, a journey of development and growth in the Spirit who fills and animates the church. The Spirit will manifest himself differently but in a growing way according to the different stages of this development toward maturity. This process has an end-point, a climax. This is when the young person begins to become capable of making his or her own life decisions, capable of being the subject of his or her own life. This stage will usually be arrived at somewhere in mid-teenage. Now the young person is capable of being a mature member of the church. The natural process of initiation, of development in the faith, is now over.

The question is how the sacraments of initiation—baptism, confirmation, first communion—should be related to this natural process of initiation into the church and development in the faith. Unless there is some realistic coherence between the sacramental system and the natural process, the initiation sacraments will lack a sense of reality and appear somewhat artificial. The view which advocates that in the context of infant baptism the initiation sacramental system should be modeled as closely as possible on the RCIA program, and the practice of the early church, involves in my view precisely this defect. On the other hand, by following and applying what I have here called the principle of realistic coherence, one can devise an initiation sacramental system which is both theologically valid and, at least in most circumstances today, pastorally effective. The system I have in mind, bearing in mind the context of infant baptism and leaving aside the special RCIA program, would be as follows: baptism in infancy; first communion as at present (or more or less); confirmation somewhere in mid-teenage.

The virtue of this latter view is that it establishes a realistic relation between baptism and confirmation and the natural initiation process of the young person into the faith and the church. Here both baptism and confirmation would retain their natural initiation character. They would frame the natural initiation period and process, providing it at its beginning and end with an appropriate sacramental context and expression. The age for first communion could here be left untouched on the ground that from this age on full participation in the eucharist is an important element in the young person's growth in faith. In such a system these sacraments would be realistically, significantly and coherently related to the natural life process and in so doing they would retain, despite the interval of years, their own intimate relationship and complex unity as sacraments of initiation. Of all the many options proposed, this I consider the most appropriate and effective setting and age for confirmation in our circumstances today.

The Spirit in the Church

A basic implication of the assessment which I have been attempting to sketch in this essay is that the way we see and understand the sacrament of confirmation depends on how we understand the church and the Holy Spirit. Confirmation is a sacrament of initiation whereby the candidate is incorporated into the church. The church expresses its being, what it is, in its initiation sacraments. Confirmation is also the sacrament of the Holy Spirit. The themes of Spirit and church thus form the essential theological context for an understanding of confirmation. The relation of these themes is thus of vital significance for the theology of confirmation.

A surprising feature of much writing on confirmation is that it so often contains little or no significant reference to the Holy Spirit. This surely is *Hamlet* without the Prince! In the western or latin church the theology of the Holy Spirit is for various historical reasons underdeveloped. The intimate relationship of the themes of Spirit and church, so obvious in the New Testament and the patristic tradition, urgently needs to be revived.

In the Creed we profess belief in the Holy Spirit *in* the holy Catholic Church, that is, as the animating principle and inspiring force which establishes and maintains this community we call church. Yet only too often the models or ways in which we traditionally think about the church have little or no overt reference to the Spirit. This is a situation which calls for comment—and for revision.

For example, when we think of church the image or model of institution is often prominent in our minds. No doubt there is reference here to a basic aspect of the church. But it does not say everything, and in itself it is a rather static and juridical image. To balance and complement it we need a concept of church as event, as something that is not just there, ever the same, but as something dynamic, ever happening, coming into existence in all kinds of wonderful ways every new day and moment. The Holy Spirit is the animating inspiring presence and dynamic force which constantly makes and remakes the church. The church is holy because the Holy Spirit by his presence in it makes it holy.

This dynamic character of the Spirit's presence is a prominent emphasis in St. Paul. All his references to the Holy Spirit are concerned with the life of the Christian community and its members. One has but to read as one whole those great chapters of 1 Corinthians 12 and 13 to see this. Some well-known texts from Romans strike the same note.

> The love of God is poured into our hearts through the Holy Spirit who has been given to us (Rom 5:5).

> The law of the Spirit of life in Christ Jesus has set me free (Rom 8:2).

> All who are led by the Spirit of God are sons of God (Rom 8:14).

The life of Christian charity is the achievement of the Holy Spirit working in us. In Galatians 5:25 St. Paul sums up his thought succinctly:

If we live by the Spirit, let us also walk by the Spirit.

This "walking by the Spirit" issues in the fruits of the Spirit:

> The fruit of the Spirit is love, joy, peace, patience, kindness, goodness, faithfulness, gentleness, self-control; against such there is no law (Gal 5:22–23).

These fruits are the personal qualities which should characterize the person and life of the Christian. They are the qualities which often enough, if we had the eyes to see, we can see developing in the young person growing in the faith, growing in and toward the fullness of the Spirit.

This context of the Spirit in the church is the context of the sacrament of confirmation. An understanding of the sacrament invites us to develop a living theology and understanding of the Spirit's presence in the church and its members, and especially in the lives of its young members, and to develop a pastoral, sacramental practice which can effectively implement that understanding. If we could but achieve that task, many of our difficulties with the sacrament of the Spirit would, I believe, be resolved and disappear. And our own Christian lives would be profoundly enriched.

Chapter 2

A CASE FOR ADOLESCENT CONFIRMATION

Kieran Sawyer, S.S.N.D.

This article is set in the context of the ongoing dialogue concerning the placement of confirmation in the initiation process, the dialogue between the "restored sequence" position and the "delayed confirmation" position. Those who hold the former position advocate that the sacrament of confirmation be restored to its original place in the initiation sequence, after baptism and before eucharist. Those who hold the latter position advocate delaying confirmation until after first eucharist for pastoral and catechetical reasons.

In support of their position, the restored sequence theologians often use passages from the RCIA, particularly Par. 215, (Par. 34 in the 1976 edition of the ritual). I attempt to show that there is also support in the RCIA, as well as in other recent church documents, for the delayed confirmation position.

I present eight initiation principles drawn from an analysis of the recent ecclesial documents that make reference to initiation. I then use the principles to shed light on some of the key issues in the confirmation dialogue, particularly the sequence question.

The documents studied include four Vatican II documents: the Constitution on the Liturgy (SC), the Dogmatic Constitution on the Church (LG), the Decree on the Church's Missionary Activity (AG), and the Decree on the Ministry and Life of Priests (PO); the three initiation rites and the decrees that accompany them: the Rite of Christian Initiation of Adults (RCIA), the Rite of Baptism for Children (RBC), the Rite of Confirmation (RC), and the General Introduction to Christian Initiation (GI); and two legal documents: the revised Code of Canon Law (CL) and the National Statutes for the Catechumenate (NSC).

Eight Initiation Principles

The Process Principle: **Christian initiation is the process by which a person comes to mature faith within the community of Christians.**

The initiation documents make it clear that initiation is not so much a once-for-all event as it is a process. In the documents, this initiation process is variously called a "spiritual journey" (RCIA 5), "a training period for the whole of Christian life" (AG 14), an "apprenticeship" (AG 14, CL 788:2), a "progressive change of outlook and conduct" (RCIA 75), and a period of pastoral and catechetical formation (RCIC 252, RBC 3). The process is divided into distinct stages (CL 851), steps (RCIA 6), or levels (RCIA 79) which are marked by various rituals.

The initiation process includes many factors: coming to know and believe in Jesus and his teachings, developing a sense of belonging or at-home-ness in the Christian community, learning to live by the values and attitudes that motivate the community, and joining in the prayer and ministry of the group (RCIA 6–9). The documents indicate that initiation takes time, even several years (RCIA 76 and 252), and that the process both precedes the sacramental ritualization and continues after it (RCIA 244, RBC 3–7).

The documents outline two parallel initiation processes— one for adults (and children of catechetical age), the other for infants. The initiation process for adults, which is considered the paradigm, is spelled out in detail in the RCIA. This process moves from evangelization, to conversion, to catechesis, to deepened conversion, to reception of the initiation sacraments, to full Christian living. The initiation process for persons baptized as infants is outlined (sketchily) in the RBC and the RC. This process begins with baptism and moves through a gradual period of faith formation designed to lead the children to "accept for themselves the faith in which they have been baptized" (RBC 3), to "give the witness of a Christian life" (RC 12), and "to spread and defend the faith" (CL 879).

The Rites Principle: There is an intrinsic coherence between the initiation rites and the initiation process.

It is important to maintain both the distinction and the interrelationship between the process by which a person comes to mature faith and the rituals that celebrate the process. The initiation rituals highlight various aspects or stages of the process. The rituals give focus to the stages and mark the passage from one to another.

While the rituals are essential to the process, they are, nevertheless, secondary to the process. The rituals presuppose an already present faith (SC 9, 59). They require the understanding, conversion, and desire that result from the process (e.g. RCIA 37, 42, 119, 292). The documents indicate that the rituals are to "suit" the process and should be adapted to the spiritual journey of those who celebrate them (RCIA 5, 35). Care is to be taken "to exclude any semblance of mere formality" (RCIA 122) in celebrating the rituals.

The liturgical rituals not only express faith, they also nourish and strengthen the faith they express (SC 59). The rites help the initiates on their journey, deepen their resolve, and complete their conversion (RCIA 75, 141).

The relationship of the initiation rituals to the initiation process is multifaceted and poetic rather that direct and specific. The one rite of Christian initiation is made up of an intricate web of related ritual actions and symbols. There is seldom a sharp delineation between the meanings conveyed by the separate rituals or between the layers of meaning within a given ritual. Meanings interconnect and overlap; they focus now on one aspect now another of the total mystery of incorporation into the body of Christ.

Pre-eminent among the rituals which mark the initiation process are the three initiation sacraments—baptism, confirmation, and eucharist. Canon 842 states that these three are "so interrelated that they are required for full Christian initiation."

In the case of adult baptism, the unity of the three initiation

sacraments is to be signified by celebrating them in a single liturgical celebration (RCIA 215, CL 866). This temporal unity does
not apply to infant baptism, however, since the documents state
that infants are to be baptized as soon as possible after birth (CL
867), while confirmation and eucharist are not to be conferred
until at least the age of discretion (CL 891, 914).

The documents always mention the three initiation sacraments in the traditional sequence (baptism, confirmation, eucharist), and it is presumed that they are to be received in that order.
(Three slight exceptions can be noted: 1. RCIA 24 makes allow-
ance for celebrating confirmation on Pentecost Sunday after the
period of post-baptismal catechesis. 2. Canon 777 mentions eucharist before confirmation when it speaks of the pastor's duty to
prepare children for the sacraments. 3. Canon 914 interrupts the
traditional sequence by interjecting sacramental reconciliation
before first eucharist.) The most recent document, the National
(U.S.) Statutes for the Catechumentate, specifically prohibits allowing children catechumens to receive the three sacraments "in
a sequence other that that determined in the ritual of Christian
initiation" (NSC 19).

The Freedom Principle: **The sacraments of initiation must be
received freely.**

Several of the initiation documents speak of the freedom
required in Christian initiation. Vatican II's Decree on the
Church's Missionary Activity (Ad Gentes) states: "The church
strictly forbids forcing anyone to embrace the faith, or alluring or
enticing people by unworthy techniques" (AG 13).

The freedom principle is expressed frequently in the RCIA,
most clearly in paragraphs 120 and 211: "With deliberate will
and enlightened faith they [the initiates] must have the intention
to receive the sacraments of the church, a resolve they will express
publicly in the actual celebration of the rite [election]" (RCIA
120). "Adults [are to] come forward of their own accord and
with the will to accept God's gift through their own belief"
(RCIA 211).

That the sacraments of initiation are to be celebrated freely is
also emphasized in canon law. Initiates must "ask to be incorpo-

rated into the church by explicit choice" (CL 206:1); ". . . persons can be admitted to the reception of baptism when they freely request it" (CL 787:2); persons are to be admitted to the catechumenate "who have manifested a willingness to embrace the faith in Christ" (CL 788).

Freedom does not preclude formation, however. The documents lay down detailed formation prerequisites that must be met before one is allowed to celebrate the initiation sacraments. (See Readiness Principle below.) A detailed formation process is seen not as negating but as enhancing the freedom of the participants.

The freedom principle becomes problematic, of course, when we consider infant baptism. The Rite of Baptism for Children states that the rite is specifically intended for those "who have not yet reached the age of discernment and therefore cannot have or profess personal faith" (RBC 1). The RBC makes clear that infants are baptized with a view to a later time when they will be able to make a free commitment to the faith. The document states that in order to "fulfill the true meaning" of infant baptism, baptized children are to be given formation that will lead them gradually to "accept for themselves the faith in which they have been baptized" (RBC 3).

The initiation of children of catechetical age also poses a freedom problem. The RCIC requires that children entering the initiation process have some degree of freedom, although the document acknowledges the limitations on their freedom that come from the strong influence of their parents, companions, and social surroundings (252). The document expects the children to seek Christian initiation either on their own initiative or at the discretion of their parents (RCIC 252). It explicitly states that the sacraments are to be conferred only on those children whose "intention" and "dispositions" make them fit to take part (RCIC 277).

The Faith Principle: **The goal of Christian initiation is mature faith.**

Baptism is, above all, the sacrament of faith. In the words of the General Introduction to the initiation rites, "the Church believes that it is its most basic and necessary duty" to inspire catechumens, parents, godparents, and all of those involved with the initiation process, to "enter into or confirm their commitment" to gospel faith. According to the Introduction, the goal of the entire initiation process—the instruction, preparation, and celebration—is "to enliven such faith" (GI 3).

Initiation celebrates both the faith of the church and the personal faith of the individual initiates. When the initiates are adults, the focus of the initiation experience is placed largely on the faith of the individual. Thus in RCIA 211 we read: "The faith of those to be baptized is not simply the faith of the Church, but the personal faith of each one of them." When the initiates are infants, the focus is primarily on the faith of the church. RBC 2 states that "children are baptized in the faith of the Church. This faith is proclaimed for them by their parents and godparents, who represent both the local Church and the whole society of saints and believers."

Whether the initiates are adults or infants, however, the goal of Christian initiation is mature faith, faith which is "strong" (RCIA 76), "enlightened" (120), "living" (211), and "committed" (211). According to the documents, mature faith is lived out in a total Christian way of life which includes meditation on the gospels, sharing in the eucharist, and doing the works of charity (75, 244). It recognizes an obligation in conscience (252) and is committed to witnessing to Christ and to spreading and defending the faith (CL 892).

Adult initiation requires that this spirit of faith be developed before the celebration of the sacraments of initiation (RCIA 120, 336). Infant baptism, on the other hand, which is meant specifically for persons who cannot yet have or profess personal faith (RBC 1), requires the commitment of the adult community to ongoing faith formation after baptism (RBC 3–7). Canon law (868) states that baptism is to be delayed unless there is a "founded hope" that this formation will take place.

The Readiness Principle: **The fruitful celebration of the initiation rituals requires readiness on the part of the participants.**

Readiness for sacraments is one of the basic themes of the Constitution on the Sacred Liturgy which states that "full, conscious, and active participation in liturgical celebrations is demanded by the very nature of the liturgy" (SC 14). To ensure such knowing, active participation, the various initiation documents spell out detailed readiness requirements for each of the rites.

The readiness requirements for *adult baptism* are clearly stated in Canon 865:1: "To be baptized it is required that an adult have manifested the will to receive baptism, be sufficiently instructed in the truths of the faith and in Christian obligations, and be tested in the Christian life by means of the catechumenate; the adult is also to be exhorted to have sorrow for personal sin."

The adult initiation process described in the RCIA includes periodic evaluation of the readiness of the initiates. The catechumenate is seen as a time of "probation" (76). Pastors, catechists, deacons, and sponsors are said to share in the responsibility of "judging" (43, 119) the progress of the candidates. The church is expected to "decide on the catechumens' suitableness" (122) and the community is asked to "express its approval" (125) before the initiates are chosen to move on to the next step in the process.

The readiness requirements for *infant baptism* are directed toward the adults involved in the initiation rather than the initiates themselves: "The parents of an infant who is to be baptized and likewise those who are to undertake the office of sponsor are to be properly instructed in the meaning of this sacrament and the obligations which are attached to it" (CL 851:2). RBC 5 describes the preparation needed to ensure that the parents take part in the rite with understanding: "They should be provided with suitable means such as books, instructions, and catechisms written for families. The parish priest should make it his duty to visit them, or see that they are visited . . . and prepare them for the coming celebration with pastoral counsel and common prayer."

The requirements for the baptism of *children* of catechetical age are spelled out in the RCIC, which states explicitly that "before the children are admitted to the sacraments at Easter, it should be established that they are ready for the sacraments" (256). The RCIC places readiness requirements on both the children and the participating adults. The children are required to have "a conversion that is personal and somewhat developed, in proportion to their age" (252); the parents are required to give permission for the children to be initiated and to live the Christian life; and the community is required to provide catechetical instruction in a supportive setting (252–254).

During the course of the children's initiation, "the Church judges their state of readiness and decides on their advancement" (278). The decision to admit the children to the next step in the process is based on their own reaffirmation of their intentions and the testimony of their parents, godparents, and catechists (278). In the rite of election, for example, the involved adults are asked if the children have shown a sincere desire to receive the sacraments, have listened well to the word of God, have tried to live as faithful followers of God, and have taken part in the community's life of prayer and service (283).

The readiness required for the *first eucharist* of children baptized in infancy is stated in Canon 913: "For the administration of the Most Holy Eucharist to children, it is required that they have sufficient knowledge and careful preparation so as to understand the mystery of Christ according to their capacity, and can receive the Body of the Lord with faith and devotion." (Canon 914 seems to add sacramental reconciliation to the prerequisites for first eucharist.) Children in danger of death need only be "able to distinguish the Body of Christ from ordinary food and to receive Communion reverently" (913).

The readiness requirements for *confirmation* are found in Canon 889:2: "Outside the danger of death, to be licitly confirmed it is required, if the person has the use of reason, that one be suitably instructed, properly disposed, and able to renew one's baptismal promises." RC 12 adds to this list the requirement that one "be in the state of grace."

Both documents set the minimum age for confirmation at about the seventh year (RC 11) or the age of discretion (CL 891). However, both also indicate the possibility of setting a later age. RC 11 gives the rationale for this delay: "For pastoral reasons, especially to strengthen the faithful in complete obedience to Christ . . . episcopal conferences may choose an age which seems more appropriate, so that the sacrament is given at a more mature age after appropriate formation." This statement would seem to include, as a requirement for confirmation, a degree of faith maturity.

The Community Principle: Initiation is the responsibility of the entire Christian community.

The documents state repeatedly that initiation is to take place within the community of the faithful. RCIA 9, for instance, says that initiation is "the responsibility of all the baptized," that "all the followers of Christ have the obligation of spreading the faith according to their abilities," and hence that "the entire community must help the [initiates] throughout the process of initiation."

Vatican II's Decree on Priestly Ministry designates "the formation of a genuine Christian community" as one of the primary tasks of the parish priest and states that the parish community "must regard as its special charge those under instruction and the newly converted" (PO 6).

The first role ascribed to the initiating community is the ministry of welcoming: "They should show themselves ready to give the candidates evidence of the spirit of the Christian community and to welcome them into their homes, into their personal conversation, and into community gatherings" (RCIA 9). Such community involvement is meant to assure that "right from the outset the catechumens will feel that they belong to the people of God" (AG 14, see also NSC 4).

The members of the community are to continue to be actively involved throughout the initiation process: they provide an example of a true Christian lifestyle, assist in evangelization and catechesis, sustain the initiates in moments of hesitancy and anxiety, help to judge the progress of the candidates, and take an active part in the various ritual celebrations (RCIA 9–11).

The participation of the community in the initiation process is expected to have a positive impact on the community as well as the initiates. The faithful "should derive from it a renewal of inspiration and outlook" (RCIA 246).

The role of the community is especially important in the

initiation of infants and children. The documents point out that "the faith in which children are baptized is not the private possession of the individual family, but it is the common treasure of the whole church" (RBC 4). "Before and after the celebration of the sacrament, the child has a right to the love and help of the community" (ibid).

The RCIC points out that, besides the adult community, children of catechetical age who are being prepared for baptism also need the help and example of a group of their peers. "[T]heir initiation progresses gradually within the supportive setting of this group of companions" (RCIC 254).

The Eucharistic Principle: The culmination of the initiation process is the eucharist.

Eucharist is the culmination and climax of the total initiation process, the summit toward which all initiation activity has been directed (RCIA 217 and 243, RCIC 329). Eucharist is the center of the whole Christian life (LG 11, SC 10, RCIA 243), "the very heartbeat of the congregation of the faithful" (PO 5).

It is clear from the documents that the phrase "culmination in eucharist" encompasses much more than simply partaking of the sacred elements. Through the reception of eucharist, the faithful "are fully joined to the body of Christ" (PO 5). Receiving communion is a sacramental sign of the initiate's full "communion" with the church. This sacred action symbolizes both the passive and the active inclusion of the individual in the community of Christians.

According to the documents, it is not only the initiation sacraments which culminate in eucharist, but all of the other sacraments as well. "The other sacraments, as well as every ministry of the church and every work of the apostolate, are linked with the holy eucharist and directed toward it" (PO 5, SC 10). (Note that eucharist is seen as the goal of even the sacraments that are celebrated later. Confirmation could thus be said to "culminate in eucharist" whether it precedes or follows first communion.)

Unlike baptism and confirmation, eucharist is not a one-time-only sacrament. The third sacrament of initiation is not "first communion" but eucharist, a sacrament which the Christian celebrates again and again. In a very real sense, each reception of eucharist "completes" initiation; each is a sign of the ongoing commitment of both the individual and the community to live the eucharistic life.

The Catechesis Principle: **Catechesis for the initiation sacraments takes place before, during, and after the celebration of the sacramental rituals.**

Canon 777 requires that "suitable catechesis [be] given for the celebration of the sacraments." The National Statutes for the Catechumenate expand this requirement, stating that "a thoroughly comprehensive catechesis on the truths of Catholic doctrine and moral life . . . is to be provided" (NSC 7).

"Catechesis," as the term is used in the documents, carries a much broader meaning than its derivatives "catechism" and "catechetics." The catechesis called for throughout the documents is not limited to instruction, but includes learning to live, believe, think, pray, witness, and minister as a Christian. The documents present in detail the catechesis that is to take place— before, during, and after the actual celebration of the various rituals—to ensure that the sacraments are celebrated "knowingly, actively, and fruitfully" (SC 11).

The chief emphasis, however, is placed on the catechesis which precedes the rites. This is detailed particularly in AG 14, RCIA 75–78, 139, and 141–142, RC 12, and RBC 5. The many catechetical elements listed in these passages fit into several categories:

- formation in faith, spirituality, and prayer;
- participation in scripture study and liturgical celebrations;
- review and reform of personal lifestyle and morality;
- involvement in the life, prayer, and ministry of a community of Christians;
- instruction in dogma and doctrine.

Secondly, the documents indicate that catechesis is to hap-

pen during the rites. The rites themselves play a role in the catechesis of both the initiate and the community: "Because they are
signs they also instruct. . . . It is therefore of capital importance
that the faithful easily understand the sacramental signs" (SC
59). Details for making the initiation rites richly instructive can
be found, for instance, in GI 18–30.

Finally, the documents call for catechesis which follows the
celebration of the initiation sacraments. This post-baptismal catechesis, called mystagogia in the RCIA, is meant to strengthen
the newly baptized "as they begin to walk in newness of life"
(RCIA 244). The components of post-baptismal catechesis include: "closer ties" with the community, a "fuller and more effective understanding" of the paschal mystery, "meditation on
the Gospel, sharing in the Eucharist, and doing the works of
charity" (RCIA 244–251, RCIC 330).

The Initiation Principles and the Confirmation Dialogue

In the current dialogue concerning the sacrament of confirmation, three major questions continue to surface: the meaning
of confirmation, the most appropriate age for celebrating confirmation, and the place confirmation should hold in the sequence
of initiation sacraments. I am convinced that the three problems
are at root one problem and that the initiation principles outlined
above help us to understand, if not to resolve, that problem.

The core problem, as I understand it, has to do with sequence. There is an intrinsic sequence inherent in the initiation
process. This sequence is presented in detail in the RCIA which
outlines a spiritual journey that takes an adult from evangelization, to conversion, to full catechesis, to deepened conversion,
to sacramental ritualization, to lived Christianity within the
community.

This initiation process is marked by a series of initiation rituals, three of which, baptism, confirmation, and eucharist, have
the status of sacraments. The sequence of the initiation *rituals*
reflects the primary sequence of the initiation *process*. The traditional ordering of the sacraments that puts baptism and confir-

mation before eucharist mirrors a primary order that puts the total baptismal reality of evangelization, conversion, and catechesis before the total eucharistic reality of full incorporation into the body of Christ.

The three initiation sacraments serve as a bridge between the process of initiation and the daily living out of the eucharistic commitment which is expected to follow the ritual celebration. Baptism and confirmation belong to the initiation process and naturally precede eucharist which is the core of the full Christian life into which one is being initiated. Baptism-confirmation-eucharist is the "correct" sequence because it suits the process by which an adult comes to mature faith in the church.

However, the intrinsic sequence that begins with evangelization and culminates in eucharist applies only to the initiation of adults. The baptism of infants, which puts the baptismal ritual before the evangelization/conversion/catechesis process, is a radical disruption of the sequence. Infant baptism sets the child on a faith journey that is radically different from that experienced by an adult convert. The question becomes: how to maintain the essential unity of process and ritual when the initiation process has been radically altered.

A close study of the church's official initiation documents reveals three different ways of dealing with the initiation of infants and children. I refer to these as the canonical approach, the RCIC approach, and the RBC approach. The three approaches are somewhat disconnected from and inconsistent with one another, and each of them is in some way in conflict with the initiation principles established by the adult paradigm. None of them is fully successful in resolving the conflict between process and ritual.

In the first approach, which I call "canonical" because it is laid out primarily in Canons 867 and 891, baptism is celebrated in infancy and confirmation and first eucharist in early childhood. Canon 867 obliges parents to bring their children to baptism "within the first weeks after birth." Canon 891 (also RC 11) requires that confirmation be "postponed" until the age of discretion, about age seven, at which time the child is expected to be "suitably instructed, properly disposed, and able to renew the baptismal promises" (CL 889:2). First eucharist is received at the confirmation mass: "The newly confirmed should participate in eucharist which completes their Christian initiation" (RC 13).

However, the documents do indicate that there is some question concerning a child's readiness for confirmation by age seven. RC 11 (also CL 891) provides for the possibility of selecting a "more appropriate" age for confirmation, so that the sacrament can be given "at a more mature age after appropriate formation." No indication is given as to when eucharist would be celebrated if this option were chosen.

The RCIC approach, which applies only to children who have for some reason attained the use of reason without being baptized, celebrates all three sacraments of initiation in one ceremony after a lengthy formation process adapted from the RCIA. A section of the RCIA (#252–330, often referred to as the Rite of Christian Initiation for Children, or RCIC) spells out the details of adapting the RCIA process for use with children.

Accommodations to the youth of the initiates are made throughout the RCIC, e.g.: "The Christian initiation of . . . children requires a conversion that is personal and somewhat developed, in proportion to their age" (RCIC 253), and ". . . the condition [for celebrating the penitential rite] is that the children are approaching the maturity of faith and understanding requisite for baptism" (RCIC 292). Nonetheless, the document states that children are not to be baptized until they have "completed their Christian initiation" (RCIC 330) and it can be "established that they are ready for the sacraments" (RCIC 256).

There is an internal conflict in the RCIC approach regarding the readiness of the children for full initiation. The document seems to expect an adult-level faith response of children who, in the words of the RCIC itself, "cannot yet be treated like adults because, at this stage of their lives, they are dependent on their parents or guardians and are still strongly influenced by their companions and their social surroundings" (252).

In the third approach, baptism is celebrated in infancy, first eucharist (and reconciliation) in early childhood, and confirmation in late adolescence or young adulthood. This approach is outlined in the Rite of Baptism for Children, especially RBC 3,

and is implied in the canons concerning first eucharist and reconciliation (CL 777, 913, 914) and in much of the language found
in the Rite of Confirmation (especially RC 11 and 12).

Much contemporary discussion has focused on the desirabil-
ity of bringing the initiation of children in line with the RCIA
paradigm. The focus of these discussions has often been on restoring the sequence of the initiation rituals. Since this goal is accomplished by the first two approaches above, some current writers
advocate that diocesan policies be adapted to incorporate these
approaches. They recommend that all children who were baptized as infants receive confirmation and first eucharist at about
age seven, and that any children age seven or older who are coming to baptism for the first time receive the other two sacraments
of initiation along with baptism.

My problem with both of these approaches is that they restore the traditional sequence of the rituals at the cost of a much
more important principle—the principle which calls for an intrinsic coherence between the initiation rites and the initiation
process. In both the canonical approach and the RCIC approach,
I believe that children are fully initiated ritually before they are
capable of completing the initiation process.

Having spent my entire adult life dealing with children and
adolescents, I am convinced that a child is simply not capable of
moving through the evangelization/conversion/catechesis process described in the documents. The "discretion" of the seven
year old child is far from the full awareness and commitment
spelled out by the documents as a prerequisite for ritual initiation. The child's ability to make or renew the baptismal promises
falls far short of the free commitment to a Christian life envi-
sioned in the RCIA.

Even in the best of circumstances, young children who have
been prepared for confirmation or those who have gone through
the catechumenate are still likely to be far from the mature, fully-
committed faith outlined in the paridigmatic RCIA. Even
though they have received the initiation sacraments, such children will not be fully initiated. They will continue to need the
kind of ongoing faith formation described in the RBC, formation
aimed at leading them to a true appropriation of the faith.

When we pay less attention to restoring the traditional sequence of the rituals, and take as our primary principle the unity of process and ritual, then the value of the RBC approach to the initiation of children becomes apparent. This approach looks first at the actual process by which a child baptized in infancy comes to mature faith, and adapts the sequence of the initiation rituals to suit that process.

In the RBC approach, the sequence of the three initiation sacraments is baptism (reconciliation), first eucharist, and confirmation. This sequence suits the initiation process by which the person who was baptized as an infant comes to adult faith. In this approach, the sacraments are celebrated at the time best calculated to advance the faith formation process of the child who is growing up within a Catholic Christian family.

The RBC process is not spelled out in the documents with anything like the detail given in the RCIA for the adult process, but a clear outline for the process is found there, especially in RBC 3 and RC 12. The initiation process described there moves from infant baptism (community commitment, RBC 2), to evangelization and catechesis (faith formation, RBC 3–5), to conversion (gradual appropriation: "accept for themselves" RBC 3), to adult faith (commitment to a eucharistic life style, RC 12), to apostolic faith (willingness to spread and defend the faith, LG 11, CL 879).

(In other articles, I call this process the RBC model of initiation in contrast to the RCIA model which is outlined in the RCIA. I hold that the two models are equally authoritative, since both are based on official ecclesial documents. The models parallel one another and mutually complement one another. Both build on the initiation principles outlined in this article. The RCIA is the "paradigm" because the goal of initiation is adult faith, not because the RCIA model is the only or best path to arrive at adult faith. For a more detailed explanation of the RBC model see my article "Readiness for Confirmation," *Living Light* 24, June 1988, 331–339.)

In this view, the baptism, eucharist, confirmation sequence is seen as a Spirit-led cultural development in sacramental practice. The sequence has developed over the centuries in the western church in response to the changing process by which children of Christian families move from socialized faith into personally committed faith.

The unity of the initiation sacraments is found in their connection to the total initiation process rather than in their temporal proximity. Baptism and confirmation frame the one initiation process. The preparation for and celebration of first communion (preceded by first reconciliation) are part of the lengthy formation process between the two initiation sacraments.

While all of the initiation rituals together carry the one meaning of incorporation into Christ, the individual rituals focus on the specific meanings that highlight one or other part of the process. Thus infant baptism focuses on the faith of the church and the gift dimension of the initiation reality, while confirmation focuses on the personal faith of the individual and the commitment dimensions of initiation.

The RBC Approach: Three Rituals, One Process

Now let us take a closer look at the three initiation sacraments as separate rituals in the one RBC process. The first of these, the one most clearly seen as a direct parallel to the RCIA, is the RBC itself. The RBC is an entirely new rite, created in response to the Vatican II mandate that "the rite of baptism for infants . . . should be adapted to the circumstances that those to be baptized are, in fact, infants" (SC 67).

Accordingly the Rite of Baptism for Children is specifically designed to initiate "children or infants . . . who have not yet reached the age of discernment and therefore cannot have or profess personal faith" (RBC 1, SC 67). The focus of the RBC is not so much on the child as it is on the parents and the adult community in whose faith the child is baptized. The rite calls on these adults to make a public commitment to the faith formation of the child they have presented for baptism. The parents' commitment is even considered a prerequisite for the baptism (CL 868).

The second initiation sacrament in the RBC model of initiation is "first communion." The first reception of the eucharist has, over the years, taken on the status of a separate initiation rite, not only in the minds of the faithful, but also in canon law. Canons 777, 913, and 914 specify the readiness required for this sacrament—"suitable catechesis," "sufficient knowledge and careful preparation," "faith and devotion"—and indicate that it is to be received "as early as possible" by children who have reached the use of reason. The canons specify that first communion should be preceded by "sacramental confession" (914) and seem to imply that it will be followed by confirmation (777).

The third initiation sacrament in the RBC model is confirmation. The Prenotanda for the Rite of Confirmation (the Decree and Apostolic Constitution signed by Paul VI) envisions confirmation as a separate ritual that completes the initiation process: "Thus [in confirmation] the initiation in the Christian life is completed so that believers are strengthened by power from heaven, made true witnesses of Christ in word and deed, and bound more closely to the church" (Decree, par 1).

The RC specifies that the preparation for confirmation should follow the principles which guide the admission of catechumens. The readiness factors of knowledge, freedom, and commitment that are given as prerequisites for adult baptism are shifted here to become prerequisites for confirmation. The RC points out that the preparation for confirmation should particularly include: "suitable catechesis," "effective relationship of the candidates with the Christian community," "formation toward . . . giving the witness of a Christian life and exercising the Christian apostolate," and "developing a genuine desire to participate in the eucharist" (12).

The internal language of the confirmation ritual also presupposes that a maturing of faith has occurred since baptism. For example, the confirmation candidates are called upon to be "more like Christ," to be "more perfect members of the Church," to be witnesses whose lives "should reflect the goodness of Christ," and to "give [their] lives completely in the service of all" (RC 22).

This same expectation of mature faith is found in Canon 879: "[Through confirmation] the baptized, continuing on the path of Christian initiation, are enriched by the gift of the Holy Spirit and bound more perfectly to the Church; it strengthens them and obliges them more firmly to be witnesses to Christ by word and deed and to spread and defend the faith."

The clearest statement linking confirmation to faith maturity is found in the "exception" clause of RC 11. "For pastoral reasons, however, especially to strengthen the faithful in complete obedience to Christ the Lord and in loyal testimony to him, episcopal conferences may choose an age which seems more appropriate, so that the sacrament is given at a more mature age after appropriate formation."

Conclusion

The baptism of infants disrupts the natural sequence of the initiation process, a process which moves from evangelization, to conversion, to catechesis, to sacraments, to Christian life. Restoring the sequence of the rituals without restoring the sequence of the process disrupts the intrinsic unity of process and ritual.

Infant baptism creates an alternate initiation process, a process that moves from the commitment of the parents, through the long years of faith formation, to the commitment of the individual. This new process requires a new sequence of the rituals. In the context of infant baptism, confirmation plays a legitimate role as the sacramental celebration of the personal faith commitment of those who have come to "accept for themselves" the faith in which they were baptized.

REFERENCES

Initiation Principles and Their Sources

The Process Principle: Christian initiation is the process by which a person comes to mature faith within the community of Christians.
(RCIA 5–9, 75; AG 13–14; CL 788, 851, 879; RC 12)

The Rites Principle: There is an intrinsic coherence between the initiation rites and the initiation process.
  (SC 59; RCIA 5, 75, 122, 141)

The Freedom Principle: The sacraments of initiation must be received freely.
  (AG 13; RCIA 120, 211; RBC 1, 3; CL 206, 787, 788)

The Faith Principle: The goal of Christian initiation is mature faith.
  (GI 3; RCIA 76, 120, 211; RBC 1–7)

The Readiness Principle: The fruitful celebration of the initiation rituals requires readiness on the part of the participants.
  (SC 14; RCIA 43, 76, 119, 122, 125, 251, 256, 278; RBC 5; RC 11–12; CL 865:1, 851:2, 889:1)

The Community Principle: Initiation is the responsibility of the entire Christian community.
  (AG 14; RCIA 9–11; RBC 1–5; PO 6; RCIC 254)

The Eucharistic Principle: Eucharist is the culmination of the initiation process.
  (SC 10; PO 5; RCIA 217, 243; RCIC 329)

The Catechesis Principle: Catechesis for the sacraments of initiation takes place before, during, and after the celebration of the rituals.
  (SC 59; GI 18–30; RCIA 75–78, 119–120, 139, 141–147, 244–251, 330; RC 12; RBC 5; CL 777; NSC 7)

Sources for the Initiation Principles

SC	Sacrosanctum Concilium, Constitution on the Sacred Liturgy, 1963	
LG	Lumen Gentium, Dogmatic Constitution on the Church, 1964	
AG	Ad Gentes, Decree on the Church's Missionary Activity, 1965	

PO   Presbyterorum Ordinis, Decree on the Ministry and Life of Priests, 1965

GI   General Introduction, Christian Initiation

RCIA Rite of Christian Initiation of Adults, 1972, 1986

RCIC Part II: 1 of the RCIA

RBC   Rite of Baptism for Children, 1969

RC   Rite of Confirmation, 1971

CL   Code of Canon Law, 1983

NSC   National Statutes for the Catechumenate, USCC, 1986

Chapter 3

TOWARD A PASTORAL THEOLOGY OF CONFIRMATION

Gérard Fourez

Many published studies, as well as the testimony of numerous priests and people responsible for religious education, give the impression that confirmation is a problem.[1] For some people it is a sacrament in search of a theology, while for others it seems to represent a theology in search of a form of celebration. This essay intends to outline a pastoral perspective for this sacrament. It suggests that, beyond historical sacramental theology and pastoral approaches to this sacrament, a look at anthropology and ecclesiology, as well as to the theology of grace, could illuminate the subject. Its main thesis is that the tension between the so-called "liturgists" (who advocate the celebration of baptism, confirmation, and eucharist in one ceremony, even for children) and the so-called "religious educators" (who advocate rituals fitting the ages of the young) can be overcome. To do so, an approach presented by L. Bouyer forty years ago can be inspiring.[2] He suggested a theology in which confirmation is not seen as the sacrament of Christian maturity. But his theology does not imply that the celebration of confirmation should not be connected with the tensions (positive and negative) lived by the church when it receives a new member. In this essay the story of Peter, Cornelius, and the early church (Acts 10–11) will be looked upon as a paradigm for a meaningful celebration of confirmation.

Several Sacraments for One and the Same Initiation

A large consensus of theologians affirms that for the initiation of an adult, baptism, confirmation, and holy eucharist have

46

to be celebrated in one and the same liturgy. Regarding baptism and confirmation, there seems to be a consensus on considering the separation of these two sacraments as the result of an historic evolution, ratified by the Council of Trent. It seems that these two sacraments have their origin in certain aspects of initiation rites, which were later separated into two celebrations. Baptism underscores the way in which a person, confronted with the historic evil, is received into a community of faith, and, by this act, introduced into the mystery of the passion and resurrection of Christ, thus experiencing the grace of God (that is, God's free love that gives us the confidence to be sons or daughters loved by this presence that Jesus called his Father and able to face the world and human history). Confirmation celebrates the gift of the Spirit thanks to which, in the course of our earthly existence, we can actually act as Jesus acted, in Christ's memory.

In the eastern church the unique character of Christian initiation has been kept, even for little children: the Christian community baptizes them, anoints them with the Spirit, and shares the eucharist with them, during one and the same ceremony. The advantage of this rite is to demonstrate that a person is received into the heart of the Christian community once and for all. It has, however, one disadvantage: it doesn't take into account the fact that the initiation of children into the Christian community requires a number of years and happens in various stages.

In the western church, the sacraments of baptism and confirmation have grown more and more separate, and a theology has been constructed to distinguish them.

In more recent times Christian communities have been confronted with the problem of celebrating the initiation of children in the process of *becoming adults*. And, naturally, they have devised celebratory rites according to this viewpoint.[3]

The thesis proposed in this article is that it would be easier to approach these questions if (a) the ecclesial aspects of the sacrament of confirmation were emphasized and (b) if we insisted more on the gift of God, and less on a commitment, sometimes understood as "moralizing" or "enrolling."

A Popular (Debatable) Theology of the Sacrament of Confirmation

To explain the current problems tied to understanding confirmation, let's consider a typical text, commonly used in the United States for the Rites of Christian Initiation of Adults (RCIA). Here is how the presider opens the initiation: "These catechumens have asked to be admitted into the sacramental life of the Church at Easter. Those who know them judge them sincere in their desire. For a long time they have heard the word of Christ and have attempted to shape their conduct accordingly. They have shared in the fellowship and prayer of their brothers and sisters. Now I wish to inform all here present of our community's decision to call them to the sacraments."[4]

This text, if it reflects well the way in which many people view the sacrament, presents two theologically disputable characteristics. First of all, it is at least "semi-Pelagian" (that is, it insists more on personal efforts than on grace). Second, it focuses the sacraments more on the people "who receive them" than on the church (the Christian community) who celebrates the sacraments.

This way of introducing the sacraments of initiation leads to an approach that one could define as "moralizing." It underscores that, to receive the sacraments, the catechumens must have conducted themselves "comme il faut" (in the proper way), and that the church is the judge of that conduct. This is an attitude in contrast to the emphasis, expressed in scripture, on the love of God, who accepts us without restriction and beyond all measure. At the bottom of this idea, there is a theology that relies more on justification by works than by faith. And good works are seen more as the result of human effort than as springing from God's gracious love, that is, grace. Those who prepare young people for confirmation know, nonetheless, that this text expresses well the prevailing climate surrounding this sacrament.

In practice, this sacrament has thus become a kind of "sacrament of Christian maturity"; young people who "receive" it are now considered adults, or at least started on the road to "maturity." Further, in this context, "to be an adult" is generally understood as "behaving according to the norms of the community of adults."

The quoted text is not only "moralizing," but it presupposes that one perceives the sacrament as focused on the person who "receives" it. It implies that the celebration focuses above all on *these* catechumens. A more traditional theology would have taken care to insist on the fact that a sacrament, even when in relation to an individual, is always a celebration of the entire Christian community: the sacraments are always celebrations "of the church." The popular theology of confirmation too often considers this a celebration of the gift of the Holy Spirit *to an individual,* while a more adequate theology would take into account the fact that, through this individual, we celebrate the gift of the Holy Spirit to the whole church and to the entire world.

In short, A. Houssiau, bishop of Liège and professor at Louvain, states it this way: "This usage makes confirmation an essential part in the process of faith development and commitment of the young Christian"[5]—and this, he notes, in spite of resistance by some theologians. Thus he recalls that, since 1952, "Father Bouyer has rejected the received ideas on the sacrament of Catholic or Christian maturity. . . . In his opinion, through confirmation, the new member of the church is marked with the seal of the Holy Spirit and consecrated in the fullness of his (her) union with the chosen people and by total participation in the spiritual life, that is, a life of communion with the body of Christ in their eucharistic celebration of the mystery of Jesus." This language does not refer to maturity or to Christian commitment.

A More Ecclesial and Less Pelagian Approach to the Rite of Initiation

In order to understand better how various theologies can lead to different approaches to the celebration, let's suggest an alternative formula to introduce the rite of initiation of adults: "These catechumens have asked to take part in the sacramental life of the church. We want to celebrate this grace and welcome them among us on this Easter night. Those who know them recognize in them the gracious and liberating love of God. They have long listened to the word of Christ and we have already seen in them the power of the Spirit. They have felt how God loves people—and especially the poor and oppressed. They have been confronted with the mystery of evil at work throughout human history, and they have taken sides. They have shared in the fellowship and in the prayers of their brothers and sisters. I wish to inform you now that our community has decided to celebrate this gift of God to our church and to share the eucharist with them."

Such a text gives another flavor to the celebration of the sacrament. It is not because we, the church, have judged them good that these people are invited to receive the sacraments. It is not by way of an ethical evaluation that the Christian assembly recognizes in them the gift of the Spirit, but by way of assessing reality, of reading a history that we recognize as holy, that is, inhabited by the Spirit. In this sacrament we celebrate the gift of God that we recognize in new Christians, even if, at the same time, we know that their histories are tied to sin, as are all of ours. The celebration is not focused on "the catechumens" but on the Christian community (that is, the church) which recognizes this gift. The object of the celebration of confirmation is the Spirit received throughout human history, and through these people. This introductory text also takes into account two elements recently underscored by John Paul II: the traditional theology of grace, and the classic affirmation that sacraments are ritual celebrations of the church and not of individuals.[6] Thus, this text seems to me to emphasize Catholic traditions relevant to confirmation better than the previously cited text, which reflects a popular but ambiguous theology.

Furthermore, this version insists on the fact that what a sacrament encapsulates during one precise moment is the gift of God that we receive throughout our existence. Confirmation is not "the" moment when one is given the Spirit, but the moment when we *celebrate* this gift: the celebration reenacts the gift and thus makes it more real, and makes us more aware of it.[7]

To Celebrate Individual Efforts at Maturity or To Celebrate the Newness of the Spirit in the Church?

The popular theology of confirmation celebrated with young people is most often focused on efforts of individuals to achieve maturity. At best, the gift of the Spirit is deemed to achieve this maturity. It follows then that the newly confirmed are supposed to do the best they can to become witnesses of the Spirit they have received. A less Pelagian approach would celebrate the Spirit received by the church in a new way, through these new members (cf. the address by John Paul II cited in note 6). This is, moreover, what a meditation on the story of Peter and the centurion Cornelius may reveal.

This account from the Acts of the Apostles shows what happens to the church when it receives pagans and new members, in whom it recognizes the power of the Spirit. At the beginning of the story, Peter and the Christian Jews "knew" perfectly what was pure and impure, good and evil. But afterward, the intrusion of the Spirit opened completely new channels to the church to the point that Peter had to justify himself in the eyes of the community. Peter had to recognize the Spirit of Christ in these pagans and so had to admit them to the church. But this admission did not only affect the pagans who were initiated into the community; the entire church was changed by that gift of the Spirit. Following this intrusion of the Spirit, the church opened itself to a pagan world of which it had been previously afraid.

An analogous situation is seen each time that a Christian community opens itself to new members. They are different, and to recognize the Spirit in them induces a change in the community. When adults convert to the faith, for example, they bring new ways of viewing things, which are going to modify profoundly the ways in which the community looks at itself and its traditions. One can also consider this phenomenon in a broader sense: the new African churches, for example, bring a fresh, new breath to our old and hardened western churches.

New members always appear somewhat like intruders who

upset the tranquillity of our old patterns. But the Christian faith
has the audacity to recognize, in these intrusions, the work of the
Spirit, just as Peter did with regard to Cornelius and his pagan
friends. And the same phenomenon of intrusion manifests itself
today each time younger generations take their place in the world
of adults.

If, despite what has been mentioned, one wishes to talk of
Christian maturity with regard to confirmation, it's necessary to
draw attention to another way of viewing maturity. When Peter
recognized in Cornelius a Christian "adult," it wasn't because he
and these pagans conformed to specific norms, but because Peter
could recognize, through faith, the Spirit that they had received.
The celebration of the gift of the Spirit thus takes on another
dimension: it leads to the recognition, through faith, of the Spirit
that is at work, although previously our eyes had beheld only
pagans.

Such a perspective gives a fuller dimension to the sacrament:
at the time of the celebration, we "mimic" the gift of the Spirit by
the gesture of the bishop imposing hands and we signify in this
way that it is through a Christian community (a church) that
people receive the Spirit. So we celebrate the gift of the Spirit to
the church. Instead of a Christian community sitting in judgment
of new members, this theology sees a new partnership rising up
because, if the new members receive the Spirit through the
church, one can say as well that the church receives the Spirit
through them. And what makes the new members "adults" is not
so much their effort, but the very fact that the community recognizes that they share in the same Spirit. The gesture symbolizing
the gift of the Spirit granted through the Christian community
(itself represented by the bishop) becomes then also the celebration of a community that recognizes that the Spirit of God expresses itself through new members.

Such a celebration is not thus uniquely centered on "those
who receive the sacrament." It is a *celebration of the whole church*.
The sacrament no longer appears to be the result of efforts sup-
plied by the "converts" (or by the young people), but it is a
celebration rejoicing in a gift that has never been earned and that
amazes us. The questions to ask "candidates" are not those that

allow us to judge them worthy of the sacrament, but to ascertain if they wish to share in the Spirit that we have received through Christ, and if they believe that the Spirit can express itself through them. In this perspective, confirmation no longer looks like a sacrament of conformity to norms of a church, but like a celebration of a new intrusion of the Spirit, in the church and in the world.

For confirmation, as for all the sacraments, the grace of God does not occur in a world without sin. In other words, grace is always a story of liberation. It is very clear in the story of Peter, mentioned above: neither he nor the first Christian communities were prepared to accept easily the presence of the Spirit among the pagans. Their vision of a Christian community was still oppressive and they wanted the new believers to adapt to Jewish culture. Neither did the pagans themselves believe that they could receive the Spirit. A similar situation can be seen in our Christian communities today. Neither adults nor young people are prepared to believe in the numerous ways in which the Spirit can manifest itself. Consequently, the church of the adults is sometimes oppressive, as is that of the young people. In such a context, celebrating the gift of the Spirit implies a great deal of mutual listening and, in the end, great discernment of different voices, so that the whole church could discern where the Spirit is leading us today. The gift of the Spirit to the church always implies the gift of tongues, the reversal of the Babel curse, the gift of the language of the heart through which the old and the young, the pagans and the Christians, men and women, the new and the old members are able to communicate.

A Renovated Preparation to Confirmation

This awareness of the theological dimensions presented above can modify preparation for confirmation. In this perspective, this preparation concerns the Christian community (who must accept the newness of the Spirit's presence) just as much as the new members (whereas practically all the booklets of preparation for confirmation deal mainly with the young people to con-

firm, and very little with the community celebrating this confirmation). The Christian community must ask itself whether it is
ready to make itself open to hear the new words that the Spirit
will address to it through the mouths of the new members. And,
in the course of their preparation, the latter will come to see that
their words and actions are not uniquely their own, but are also
stemming from the Spirit present in them. And the conversion
connected with the Christian life will no longer be seen as a condition for being accepted to the sacrament, but as the effect pro-
duced when one receives the gift of the Spirit.

In the case of confirmation of young people, this approach
can clarify many issues. In Peter's time, the danger was that
Judaeo-Christian communities would require Christians who had
been pagans to be circumcised. The danger today, perhaps, is that
adults see or appreciate young people only in terms of their own
standards. This is called "adultism," as analogous to the terms
racism, sexism, etc. "Adultism" is indeed a problem in our society that refuses to trust young people, and that continues often to
consider them as children until the time they begin professional life.

The Christian community of adults, always a bit nervous
regarding young people who are becoming autonomous and independent, is not safe from "adultism." For this reason, one
could include in the preparation for the celebration a new awareness that it is important to avoid considering these young people
as only not-yet-mature adolescents, so as to hear in them the voice
of the Spirit of God who speaks to the church and to the world. In
this way, *the adult community will learn,* as Peter did when confronted with Cornelius, how the Spirit can speak in a new language through new Christians. But the celebration equally emphasizes how it is *through the community* that *the young people
receive the Spirit.* The adult community will thus be affirmed since
the traditions that it wants to pass on to young people are recognized in sharing the same Spirit. And, as the adults recognize the
Spirit in the young people, these adolescents will see that they are
taken seriously, as people who are equal in the Spirit. By such a
celebration, as in Peter's time, a new partnership in faith can be
established among old and new members of the church, sharing

in the same multifaceted Spirit. Such celebrations will produce what they signify: the adult as well as the young person could begin to realize in the course of this process that the Spirit is present on both sides, and that it is possible to make yourself open to hearing it.

Nevertheless, the Spirit's presence is not a gift in a world without problems. As we have already emphasized, it is given in a world profoundly touched by sin. Christian sacraments are always part of a story of salvation, that is, marked by the confrontation of a loving God with a history tainted by evil. It is against this background that the Christian community learns to discern the Spirit's action. The confirmation of adolescents then could, in the pastoral plan, help generations to face each other mutually, accepting the ambiguities within each one, and recognizing in the other the presence of God. Then the sacrament of the Spirit's gift can lead to belief, in faith, that a diversity of the Spirit's manifestations can find some unity (at least eschatologically) by sharing in one fellowship.

At the time of preparation of young people, one could emphasize, on the one hand, the fact that, from this moment on, what they do and the plan of their whole life begin to be in their hands and will be seen by others as the expression of the way the Spirit speaks to them and in them. They will have to know that the celebration thus will reinforce the power of the Spirit in them. On the other hand, the preparation of the Christian community will have to lead the adults to recognize the Spirit in what these young people live (but they will also consider the way in which the Spirit is living in the adult community, which has a message to pass on to youth).

This manner of celebrating will not raise the problems that the sacrament of "Christian maturity" carries with it, when it is practically understood as a celebration of conformity with the adult group. But it can be seen as a celebration of Christian maturity if that means the mutual recognition of the Spirit, in the young people as well as in the adults.

This perspective puts the debate concerning the age of confirmation in a new light. To understand what is at stake, let us consider a conversation that I had recently with a person responsible for religious formation in a very popular parish. She was hoping to show that youngsters twelve years old were not sufficiently mature to be confirmed. To support her position, she told me what had happened the very week following the confirmation of one hundred and ten children in her parish: "One had been arrested for using drugs, one had attempted suicide, and one girl found out she was pregnant. And this after eight months of serious preparation for confirmation!" This case is undoubtedly somewhat exceptional, but every catechist knows such stories, even if they are rarely so extreme.

If one thinks in terms of "justification by works" or of moral commitment, this woman was completely right: these children were not mature enough to take up whatever attitude the adult community wished for them.

But according to the perspective presented in this article—where the *gift of God,* that is, grace, is at the basis of sacramental theology—the approach would have been different. The adults of the Christian community would not have expected that these young people behave well. The community's preparation for confirmation would have been focused on the act of "opening oneself up to the unexpected." The Christian community thus would have been better prepared to see, even in these extreme actions, not *only* transgressions and sins, but also, in quite a paradoxical way, a form of God's gift. Not that there was some way to "make right" these deviant behaviors that we qualify as evil, but because, even in the midst of such situations, as disconcerting as they may be, the Spirit calls upon us in some way and requests that we listen. If we celebrated the way—often unconscious—in which young people can "transmit" the Spirit, the community could have been lead to ask itself, for example: "What lesson do we find here, for us, in this conduct of our young people? What do their deeds tell us about this society where so many young people seem to have so much trouble finding their place?" Or, to put it another way, one could use the language of classic theology on "the specific grace of the sacraments" and so to marvel that, thanks to the preparation and to the celebration, the Christian community could receive the specific grace to see these situations not only as sinful, but also as messages by which we could encounter, in faith, the Spirit. Would it not be possible that this celebration might teach the entire community—as the best educators have learned—that deviant or rebellious behavior of young people can be very instructive for adults? Through them the whole community can be lead to conversion and to question itself on the way in which it accommodates young people. Even in sin, God calls us.

In more positive terms, one could underscore this fact, confirmed by experience: when very young adolescents share their viewpoints in a group where adults are able to hear them, they often bring an experience of God and of life that can be very enriching for the adults.

Regarding confirmation, the question thus is not to know if young people can be judged mature enough by the adult community. The question could rather be: "What age is the most appropriate to celebrate the mutual recognition of the Spirit?" Thus it is unlikely that, in our culture, we would want to celebrate the mutual gift of the Spirit with infants who can in no way be considered independent people (even if the baptism of these children can be very meaningful as it celebrates the way in which they are able, with the Christian community, to share in the love that God has for us).

It seems that, in our culture, it is around the age of twelve that relationships between young people and adults begin to change. That's the time when, on both sides, the two groups see themselves at odds with each other and begin to feel the "otherness" of the other. Then young people begin to be afraid of adults, and adults come to recognize the independence of the young people. It is also the period in which adolescents, at least if they are not yet crushed by "adultism," begin to believe in their own impact on the world. Isn't this a good time to rejoice and to celebrate our trust that these young people, like adults, can pass on the Spirit to the entire community? Isn't this a good moment for adults to get in touch with their fear of young people and their tendency not to take them seriously? Isn't this a good time to make young people aware that adults, also, are capable of receiving? Isn't it, finally, a good time for all to remember that through all these changes we can celebrate God's gift of the Spirit to each one of us? At the very time that adults and young people tend to antagonize each other, wouldn't it make sense that they be invited to a celebration that will help the adults reject "adultism" and will help the community recognize how, young people and adults, we can see, each in the other, the Spirit of God?

Would that not be, for the combined community, a good opportunity to share in a significant way the celebration of initiating the young people into the Christian community? Thus, as the pope emphasized, in celebrating confirmation the church acknowledges that it is the temple of the Spirit, the church of Pentecost. And confirmation will not be reduced to "a new profession of faith or a heightened commitment."[8]

But, in this perspective, a shift in emphasis has occurred. Instead of asking ourselves: "Do we consider these young people mature enough to make a personal commitment?" we will henceforth ask ourselves: "Are we ready to recognize together that they too have received the Spirit?" And then, in the heart of an "adultist" culture that tends to keep young people in childhood, the tradition of celebrating the Spirit can lead the church to recognize the Spirit in young generations.[9] From this perspective, after all, separation of the rites of baptism and confirmation in the global Christian initiation could be considered a very positive practice.[10]

NOTES

1. Concerning the theological and pastoral debate about confirmation, see, for example, in French: Paul De Clerck, "Confirmation et communautés de foi, pour une pastorale renouvelée," in *La foi et le temps,* 1980, no. 5, pp. 411–428; Henri Bourgeois, *L'initiation chrétienne et ses sacrements* (Croire et Comprendre) (Paris: Le Centurion, 1983); Paul De Clerck and a working team, *Confirmation et communautés de foi,* Dossiers Libres (Paris: Cerf, 1981); "La confirmation," in *Célébrer,* no. 185, Dec. 1986; and a special issue of *La Maison-Dieu,* no. 1986/4. In English: John Roberto, *Confirmation in the American Church* (a 1978 NCDD Resource Paper, Washington, 1978); Thomas A. Marsh, *Gift of Community: Baptism and Confirmation* (Wilmington: Michael Glazier, 1984); Gerard Austin, *Anointing with the Spirit* (New

York: Pueblo Pub. Co., 1985); Kieran Sawyer, *Confirming Faith* (Notre Dame: Ave Maria Press, 1982); Aidan Kavanagh, *The Shape of Baptism: The Rite of Christian Initiation* (New York, Pueblo Pub. Co., 1978) and a good number of books or articles published in magazines like *PACE, Living Light,* and *Church.* See also my books *Sacraments and Passages* (Notre Dame: Ave Maria Press, 1985) (especially the chapter devoted to confirmation) and *Good News for the World* (Kansas City: Sheed & Ward, 1986). Also, more recent but only in French: *Les sept sacraments* (Paris: Le Centurion, 1989).

2. See the dated but important articles by P. Bouyer, "Que signifie la confirmation?" in *Paroisse et Liturgie,* 34, pp. 3–12 and 65–67, 1952; La signification de la confirmation," in *Vie spirituelle, Supplément,* 29, pp. 162–179, 1954.

3. In fact, most societies do not have the equivalent of adolescence, and children reach adulthood without passing through a defined intermediate stage. Most societies, however, celebrate the passage to adulthood. But it seems that in our industrialized society we know at least two passages: that from infancy to adolescence and then from adolescence to adulthood. This increases the socio-anthropologic problem of producing rituals matching such a situation.

4. *The Rites of the Catholic Church* (New York: Pueblo Pub. Co., 1983), p. 65. The text of the Francophone ritual emphasizes the action of the Spirit a little more than the English text, but it is still moralizing and focused only on those who are "going to take a decisive step" by this sacrament: "Christian brothers and sisters, these catechumens have affirmed their desire to receive, during the coming Easter, the life that the Church gives through the sacraments. For the Apostle Paul 'No one can say that Jesus is savior, if it is not by the Holy Spirit.' In addition, he adds that the Spirit acts in people 'with a view to the good of all' and that the fruit of the Spirit, love, shows itself by joy, peace, patience, and goodness. In light of this instruction, the communities of these catechumens believe they are ready to take a decisive step. For this reason, we wish to call them to the sacraments. Sponsors, do you approve now of what these catechumens are coming here to do?" Note that these texts aim at calling Christians to the entire Christian initiation, and not only to confirmation. It is the same with the episode of the centurion Cornelius, mentioned below.

5. "La redécouverte de la liturgie par la théologie sacramentaire," in *La Maison-Dieu,* 149, pp. 27–55, 1982. The articles by P. Bouyer are cited in note 1.

6. In a recent speech (March 27, 1987) the pope was clearly point-

ing to this ecclesial aspect of the celebration of confirmation. He spoke less of the individual than of the church: "It is especially in celebrating confirmation that the church acknowledges that it is the temple of the Spirit, the church of Pentecost." Likewise, speaking of confirmation, he called upon us to give priority to God's gift over the commitment of those being confirmed; he requested, indeed, that pastors "envision it as God's gift that perfects the Christian and the disciple, *without reducing it to a new profession of faith or a heightened commitment* (our emphasis) that could take its place among various stages of life" (*La Documentation Catholique,* no. 1940, 24 May 1987).

7. This is not a pure intellectual, or noetic, awareness, but an actualization of the power of God's gift. Rosemary Ruether said it well: "Authentic liturgy, which is done with real intentionality and meaning, requires a lot of energy. This means that it takes considerable time both to prepare it, and also to assimilate it afterward. Liturgy means lifting up a particular human moment, and making it paradigmatic of all moments, focusing in the mimetic reenactment of this moment all our accumulated fears and hopes for this type of event. We should properly be both exhilarated and exhausted when we have truly worshipped." See *Women-Church* (New York: Harper & Row, 1987), p. 107.

8. See note 6.

9. Later perhaps, when the young people have come of age and passed from adolescence to adulthood, there will be room to celebrate anew, in a different way, in faith, the Spirit that they will have received. There is also a theological and practical problem in countries like Belgium that have introduced ceremonies of "solemn communion" comprising renewal of baptismal vows. It is not unusual that the way in which young people are requested to "renew" their "baptismal commitments" causes discomfort, because these "commitments" do not always correspond to their situations as young people. Still, there is a lot of meaning in "renewing" baptismal rites (but obviously not in the sense of a second baptism). It would mean the entire Christian community reliving the entrance of the young people into the church, these who are now fully aware. The local church, in welcoming them, would then have to explain *how,* in its actual (concrete) history, it tries to live the gospel and to follow Jesus Christ, and to fight against the evil spirit. They would ask the young people if they wish to share in the faith, the hope, and the love in the traditions of this community. Their commitment would then take on an individual character and would take on the theological and practical dimension of sharing (participating?) in the life of the church. We could thus avoid such unilateral situations where

young people are asked to take an oath of commitment, facing adults who themselves are not saying where they stand (or who say so only in abstract and pre-historic theological expressions). Such a celebration of renewal of baptismal vows (those of the community as well as those of the new members) would then be, in the life of the parish community, a strong moment in its faith life, and not only something that is done for and by young people.

10. There remains a theological problem that is not touched on here, but that is not new: how to justify access to the eucharist before confirmation, and what theological meaning to give to a confirmation that follows the eucharist?

Chapter 4

ADOLESCENT CONFIRMATION
AND THE PASCHAL MYSTERY

Richard Reichert

The questions and concerns surrounding the sacrament of confirmation are somewhat symptomatic of the overall state of the church. They reflect the presence of two dominant ecclesiologies that are operative today. One ecclesiology, with its historical roots in the post-reformation, focuses on membership and emphasizes the need to protect its members from theological errors and the contaminating influence of society. The other ecclesiology, flowing from the Vatican II renewal, stresses the nature of the church as a community of disciples and emphasizes the need for the church to be in mission to society.

In theory, of course, both views are compatible and add to our understanding of the church. In practice, however, they can result in quite different understandings of the nature of the church as institution and the respective roles of the hierarchy and laity within the church. How one understands the mission of the church also hinges on the ecclesiology espoused. More to the point in this essay, they can lead to quite different understandings of the meaning and appropriate celebration of the sacraments of initiation into the church.

In much the same way there are several operative sacramental theologies present in the church today, each with its own emphasis. One has its roots in the liturgical renewal initiated by Vatican II. Drawing upon the practices and writings of the early church, it stresses the sacraments as mysteries with a special power and effectiveness in their own right—and consequently emphasizes the importance and power of the proper celebration of the rites. However, this liturgical approach is quite distinct from and intended to correct a too literal interpretation of the *ex opere operato* principle that became popular during the post-reformation. But the post-reformation interpretation, often in a distorted and over-simplified form, continues to be a common understanding of sacraments among many Catholics today. Finally, since Vatican II others are seeking to bring the role of culture, anthropology and sociology to bear upon our understanding of the nature and effectiveness of the sacraments.

Again, these various approaches to sacramental theology are not incompatible in theory. Each adds a valuable dimension to a wholistic understanding of sacraments. However, when any of these approaches is translated to pastoral practice in isolation from the others, contradictory conclusions result. Hence, the existence of what is often called the "confirmation debate."

These various understandings of church and sacrament all have (or should have) one thing in common. They have their origins in and seek to give living expression to the paschal mystery. If we desire to integrate and harmonize these various ecclesiologies and sacramental theologies and translate them into commonly acceptable pastoral practice regarding confirmation, it seems appropriate to reflect once again on this common source and goal. That is our purpose here.

Paschal Mystery: One Reality, Two Movements

The paschal mystery is just that—a mystery. The term designates the mysterious plan and action of God in human history, whereby we are rescued from the enslaving power of evil and God's reign is established among us. This mystery is the central message of both the Hebrew and the Christian scriptures. It is foundational to our understanding of Christ and the nature and mission of his church. Therefore, we can't hope to reduce the paschal mystery to some theological formula. But even within the limits of this short essay it is possible to identify certain key elements of the mystery that have a bearing on our concern.

From God's vantage the paschal mystery is a unity. The end intended by God is already present in its beginning. For God the concept and its completion are not separated by periods of time or by a sequence of individual acts. But we do not experience the paschal mystery nor can we fully comprehend it in such a unified way. We both experience it and therefore need to understand it as a series of distinct actions, one following upon the other.

From our limited vantage the paschal mystery is experienced and understood as two distinct (but unified) actions or movements. First, God rescues us from the enslaving forces of evil and restores us to freedom. We recognize this rescue/rebirth aspect of the paschal mystery in the Hebrews' passover/exodus experience and in Jesus' death/resurrection experience. Second, God calls and empowers us to be a priestly people, missioned to be a sign of and instrument for the establishment of the reign of God throughout all humanity. This covenanting/empowering/commissioning experience is recorded in the events surrounding the Hebrews' Sinai covenant and again in the Apostles' Pentecost as recorded in Acts.

Clearly, neither of these two actions or movements (a saving from and a covenanting/empowering for) makes sense apart from the other. They are two dimensions of a single reality, the paschal mystery. Yet they were historically experienced as two distinct moments. The authors of scripture probably used a certain liberty in giving a precise time between the two experiences which is not historically accurate (e.g. three months between the passover/exodus and the Sinai covenant; fifty days between Jesus' resurrection and the outpouring of the Spirit). But they are accurate insofar as they describe what was historically experienced as two distinct events, separated by some unspecified period of time.

Celebrating the Paschal Mystery: The Early Church

As the apostolic and then the post-apostolic church continued to reflect upon their own experience of the paschal mystery and struggled to find appropriate ways to initiate converts into its reality, they preserved both the sense of its ultimate unity and its existentially distinct movements of rescue/rebirth and empowering/commissioning. Thus evolved the rite of a water bath, followed by the laying on of hands and finally participation in the eucharist, viewed and celebrated as distinct elements of a single reality.

This unified rite reflected the theological reality they were seeking to celebrate. Because their focus was adult converts who could be expected to immediately take up an active role in the community's mission to witness to society, this practice was also pastorally valid. But there is evidence that even the early church was willing to ritually separate the water bath from the laying on of hands when practical and pastoral circumstances dictated it—such as the bishop's absence.

This is precisely the point we seek to make. Our challenge today is similar to that of the early church: achieving balance. In other words, how do we initiate people into the paschal mystery in such a way that we both preserve the theological reality of the unity of that mystery and also remain sensitive to the pastoral realities we experience? If we focus too much on one aspect at the expense of the other, we risk being ineffective in both areas.

Paschal Mystery: Steps Toward Loss of Balance

This loss of balance is precisely what did take place in varying degrees as the church moved from the post-apostolic era toward the middle ages and beyond. At the risk of over-simplifying a very complex history, we can identify three key influences which diminished this desired balance between theology and pastoral practice.

First is the development and then the popular distortion of the concept of original sin. As it became fixed in popular understanding as an objective "thing" which barred even infants from salvation and could be removed only by baptism, the effect was to destroy the sense of unity that had once existed between baptism and confirmation as sacraments of initiation into the paschal mystery. Baptism began to take on an urgency and importance of its own, apart from confirmation. Baptism also took on a more individualistic value since it was viewed as "doing something" to the individual apart from the community.

Second, this development of a theological separation between baptism and confirmation almost simultaneously led to a pastoral separation. The occasion was the church's encounter with the barbarian tribes and its desire to convert them. The gradual conversion and catechizing process practiced in the original catechumenate gave way to the practice of mass baptisms (reflecting the new-found sense of urgency to baptize) to be followed later by catechesis and confirmation. Thus the practice of separating baptism from confirmation by an indefinite period of months or even years became ingrained in the pastoral life of the church. By the middle ages theologians found it necessary to struggle to justify the very existence of confirmation and give it a theological/pastoral value sufficient to motivate the people to seek it.

Third, the *ex opere operato* aspect of sacramental theology was given such great emphasis in response to the reformation movement that in popular understanding it gradually tended to overshadow the other aspects of sacramental theology such as the role of the community and the importance of the individual's personal readiness, receptivity and faith. Applied to baptism and confirmation in isolation from the original sense of their unity and relation to the paschal mystery which the early church possessed, this excessive emphasis on *ex opere operato* further allowed baptism and confirmation to exist apart, both theologically and pastorally.

Toward Renewal

Since Vatican II liturgists have been the driving force in helping us recapture the early church's understanding of the theological unity that exists between baptism and confirmation and the restoration of unified initiation rites that reflect that reality.

The RCIA movement has done an equally valuable service in helping us understand conversion as an ongoing process and in rediscovering the essential role the community must play in the celebration of sacraments in general and the sacraments of initiation in particular. They, together with the liturgists, have also helped resituate the concept of *ex opere operato* in this larger perspective. We can never underestimate the role these contributions are playing in the overall renewal of the church.

However, if either of these developments has a weakness, it might be in the tendency to apply these restored truths without sufficient sensitivity to the pastoral realities experienced by the church today. If or when this happens, there is the danger that they could actually become obstacles to achieving the desired balance between theology and pastoral practice we seek today.

It would seem that it is precisely in this area of sensitivity to pastoral realities that the practice of adolescent confirmation has the most to contribute. Thanks to the work of liturgical renewal, the theological unity of baptism and confirmation is a given today and is reflected in most current catechetical programs related to adolescent confirmation. Thanks to the work of the advocates of the RCIA movement, those engaged in adolescent confirmation are (often painfully) aware of the critical role the community must play if their efforts are to be effective. Operating from these givens, today's youth catechists are also showing great pastoral sensitivity and creativity in their ministry. They continue to struggle to adapt their message and methods so that confirmation can make sense to young people who are in a very dynamic stage of personal development and who are often bombarded by values that run counter to the gospel. Out of pastoral necessity these catechists are seeking to draw upon the contributions that psychology, sociology and anthropology can give to our understanding of faith development and sacramental theology. There is much of value in this work.

On the other hand, if adolescent catechesis for confirmation has a weakness it is found in the danger of being too quick or indiscriminate in applying principles of psychology and anthropology to confirmation. It certainly is not being true to the paschal mystery to reduce confirmation to a "rite of passage" or to talk of it exclusively in terms of maturity or even a personal appropriation of the faith received in baptism. Such concepts can be helpful in trying to understand what takes place when someone is initiated into the paschal mystery. But confirmation signifies a reality that goes far beyond these anthropological and psychological insights.

Toward a Synthesis

Viewed both pastorally and theologically there is adequate justification for the continued practice of adolescent confirmation in today's church. Existentially, the movement of rescue/rebirth contained in the paschal mystery is distinct from the movement of empowerment/commissioning. While acknowledging the inner theological unity between the water bath and the laying on of hands, the church did evolve two distinct sacraments. When it serves a valid pastoral reality, the full meaning of the paschal mystery and intended purpose of these two sacraments can actually be enhanced when celebrated apart from each other.

So it need not be a question of either/or in the current "confirmation debate." The inner unity of the baptism/confirmation ritual followed by eucharist should certainly be normative when initiating adult converts and older children after a suitable catechumenate. But it would seem to be counter to good pastoral practice to artificially impose this ritual unity and order upon infants and children born into Catholic families. Just as Jesus warned that the sabbath exists for people and not vice versa, our sacramental rites exist for people and not vice versa.

For such infants and children it would seem more pastorally responsible to continue to allow the present ritual separation. After an infant's baptism we should therefore continue the present practice of nurturing the child's faith within the community —and at the eucharistic table—while gradually developing in her or him the knowledge, skills and motivations needed to be effective witnesses in society. At an appropriate time, to be discerned by the youth, his or her sponsor and the community, confirmation could effectively celebrate that aspect of the paschal mystery it is intended to celebrate: an empowerment by the Spirit already present in the community and a commissioning of the person to officially join the community's mission to witness in society to the saving action of God. The authentic unity and meaning of baptism/confirmation is not being threatened by such a practice. In this present moment in the church's history it can actually help support and promote the key insights that the liturgical renewal and the restored RCIA are giving to the church.

Summary

In summary, a proper appreciation for the theological meaning of the paschal mystery allows us to see both the unity and the distinctiveness of the sacraments of baptism and confirmation. It further helps us to understand the church as a community of disciples, rescued and reborn, and then empowered and commissioned for witness to society. At the same time, our pastoral sensitivity dictates that we continue to allow for a variety of ways to effectively initiate people into this mystery and into this community of disciples. Seen within this framework of the paschal mystery, adolescent confirmation definitely continues to have a rightful role as one of these theologically correct and pastorally effective ways.

II

Confirming Adolescents: Current and Future Practice

Chapter 5

CONFIRMATION AT ST. ELIZABETH'S PARISH: A REFLECTION

Arthur J. Kubick

A friend of mine recently suggested that confirmation—because of its twisting–turning history—has been one of the most "living" of the church's sacraments. The present dialogue, or, better, debate about its meaning and place in the church's life points to this vital quality. No one has a neutral opinion about confirmation. Go to any parish and ask parishioners or staff their feelings on the sacrament. Or gather liturgists, pastors and DREs together for a "simple discussion" on confirmation. Even Donahue might have trouble moderating the lively exchange.

As the church moved from generation to generation, confirmation took on new meanings. From a simple sealing or "confirming" of baptism in the early centuries to the "soldier of Christ" imagery many of us experienced seems like a giant leap. But the strands of theological thought that began with St. Paul and moved through Irenaeus, Augustine, Alcuin and Thomas Aquinas tie much of this history together. In fact, as Thomas Marsh suggested in his book *Gift of Community: Baptism and Confirmation* (Wilmington: Michael Glazier, Inc., 1984), "the Church's practice and understanding of Christian initiation has come down through the centuries shaped by the interacting history of practice and theological thought" (p. 177). This shaping makes our contemporary dialogue about the meaning and place of confirmation especially interesting and lively.

In this paper I would like to reflect on some of the elements in that dialogue. I will conclude with the experience of one parish: St. Elizabeth of Hungary in Acton, Massachusetts.

For a number of years confirmation had been dragging along

as a question-and-answer, soldier of Christ sacrament for third to sixth graders. The revised *Rite of Confirmation* (1971), along with the *Rite of Baptism for Children* (1969) and the *Rite of Christian Initiation of Adults* (1972, 1985), especially with its chapter on the Christian initiation of children of catechetical age, breathed new life into our understanding of confirmation. These texts placed confirmation squarely within the context of Christian initiation and renewed the dialogue about the meaning, hence age, of confirmation.

Today, two trends are evident in our preparation for confirmation in the United States: (1) the RCIA is becoming an important model for understanding and celebrating confirmation, and (2) the age for this celebration is moving into the mid-adolescent years (16–18). Several recent surveys bear this out. *Professional Approaches for Christian Educators (PACE) 14* (St. Mary's Press, 1983–84) published the results of a national survey done by the archdiocese of Miami. Discussing the survey, Lise M. Holash in "Confirmation in the U.S. Catholic Church" points out that in addition to moving confirmation to a higher age in most dioceses, "There is a growing consensus of a direct relationship between the implementation of the RCIA, Confirmation preparation and practice, and the quality of Christian living." A survey by the National Conference of Catholic Bishops (1984) found that mid- to late-adolescence was the preferred time for celebrating confirmation. One hundred and six dioceses responded to the survey indicating that confirmation was celebrated anywhere from grades three to twelve; the majority confirmed in eighth, ninth and eleventh grades. In the summer of 1986 Joan Eckstein surveyed the parishes of the archdiocese of Cincinnati about their confirmation practices (see "Confirmation: A Problem Sacrament," *Catechist,* January 1987, pp. 34–41). She found that Cincinnati tended to follow the national trends cited in the Miami survey but at a much slower pace. Her questions on the RCIA found that while 59% of the parishes were implementing the RCIA, only 33% modeled their confirmation preparation on it.

Publishers are certainly aware of the movement toward high school preparation and RCIA models. The confirmation materials from religious education publishers currently used in parishes bear this out. Not only do these base their vision and structure on the RCIA, they also center on high school/young adult candidates. *Be My Witnesses* (William H. Sadlier, 1985), *Water and Spirit* (Benziger, 1864, revised 1990), and *Choice* (Mahwah: Paulist Press, 1986) make the RCIA central to the confirmation process. While these three are modeled totally on the RCIA, a number of other texts incorporate some elements of the RCIA: Kieran Sawyer, *Confirming Faith* (Ave Maria, 1982); Edmund F. Gordon, *Emmaus Road* (Our Sunday Visitor, 1982); Richard Reichert, *Community of the Spirit* (Wm. C. Brown, 1982) and *Born in the Spirit of Jesus* (Wm. C. Brown, 1986); William J. Koplik and Joan E. Brady, *We Celebrate Confirmation* (Morristown: Silver Burdett, 1983); *Welcome to the Way* (Tabor, 1987). Thomas Zanzig covers both the history of confirmation and the principles for an RCIA process in the director's manual for his high school program, *Sharing the Christian Message* (St. Mary's Press, 1985). In these publications the message is clear: the RCIA is the preferred model and mid- to late-adolesence the preferred age for confirmation.

The reasons for these two trends are: Over the past ten to fifteen years we once again understand confirmation as an initiation sacrament. Thanks to both the revised confirmation rite and the RCIA our awareness of the unity of the initiation sacraments is being renewed. For the most part, we no longer see baptism, confirmation and eucharist as isolated sacraments celebrated in a vacuum. The vision of the RCIA is so comprehensive, one wonders how any of the initiation sacraments could be celebrated outside of that context. In the Cincinnati survey 33% of the parishes answered yes to the question: "Is your confirmation preparation modeled on the RCIA?" But 65% answered no. How do they prepare people for the initiation sacrament? The same question might also be asked of baptism and eucharist.

While all commentators would agree on the initiatory dimension of confirmation, they divide into several groups on the place and age for celebrating this sacrament. The "unitary-sacramental" view, rooted in the patristic initiation model of the early Christian centuries, maintains that baptism-confirmation-eucharist should be celebrated together at one time. Aidan Kavanaugh,

O.S.B., in *The Shape of Baptism: The Rite of Christian Initiation* (Pueblo, 1978) and in *Confirmation: Origins and Reform* (Pueblo, 1988); Gerard Austin, O.P., in *Anointing with the Spirit. The Rite of Confirmation: The Use of Oil and Chrism* (Pueblo, 1985) and Mark Searle, in "Confirmation: The State of the Question," *Church* (Winter 1985, 15–22), are proponents of this position. For them confirmation makes sense only in this unity because it seals or confirms baptism and sends the newly baptized to eucharist.

Opinions diverge as to the age for celebrating initiation. Some provide a rationale for full initiation in infancy followed by ongoing catechesis to adulthood. Others offer a rationale for accepting infants in the catechumenate and then initiating them in late adolescence or adulthood.

A variation of this maintains the baptism-confirmation-eucharist order but separates them by a number of years. An experiment carried out in some parishes in the United States celebrates baptism in infancy and then confirmation and eucharist together somewhere between the ages of seven to ten. See "Confirmation With First Communion? It Works!" by Terri McKenzie and Michael J. Savelesky, *Chicago Catechumenate,* now *Catechumenate: A Journal of Christian Initiation* (May 1986, pp. 16–23), and Richard Moudry, "A Parish Experience," *Catechumenate* (March 1989, pp. 44–52). In this setting neither sacrament is seen as "an entity separate from the dynamics of initiation. Eliminated is both the mentality of making one's 'first communion' and the confusion about the meaning and purpose of confirmation" (McKenzie and Savelesky, p. 19). In *Forum,* the newsletter of the North American Forum on the Catechumenate (Fall 1986), Christiane Brusselmans gives her support to this direction.

The most common pastoral practice today separates the initiation sacraments by a number of years: baptism in infancy, eucharist around ages seven or eight and confirmation sometime during the high school years. This tradition of confirmation as an independent sacrament, joined with a position of confirmation as an affirmation of faith, is the experience of most American Catholics.

In recent years the RCIA and the views of the unitary sacrament view have refined this position so that the intimate relation-ship between baptism, confirmation, and eucharist has become clearer. The celebration of confirmation has emphasized various values at various times: commitment and discipleship, witness and evangelization, strengthening through the life of the Spirit, caring for society, church membership, ongoing initiation, a sealing of baptism and a rite of dismissal. Can we maintain these perspectives on confirmation, continue to celebrate it after bap-tism and eucharist and still affirm the unity of Christian initia-tion? The ongoing dialogue about Christian initiation has pro-duced a number of creative responses. Thomas Marsh, Edward Jeremy Miller and Henri Bourgeois have observed that the ques-tion of sacramental unity is broader than mere temporal unity. Adult initiation presupposes one particular set of circumstances, infant initiation another. Infant baptism brings a person into the Christian community; the celebration of confirmation after eu-charist comes as the climax of this basic formation in faith, "the conclusion of the process which heralds entry into mature and responsible membership of the Church" (Marsh, *Gift,* p. 191). Baptism and confirmation frame the initiation process of a per-son baptized in infancy and confirmed in late adolescence. To-gether they constitute one full rite of initiation.

To this understanding of confirmation Edward Jeremy Miller adds "ecclesial commissioning." In his article, "Confir-mation as Ecclesial Commissioning," *Louvain Studies* 10 (Fall 1984, 106–121), he argues for celebrating confirmation "at an age when responsibility can be assumed," because it is a commis-sioning for ministry, an ordination to shape the future of both the church and the world.

For Henri Bourgeois, in *On Becoming Christian: Christian Initiation and Its Sacraments* (Twenty-Third Publications, 1985), memory and time add important dimensions to the initiation process. He sees confirmation "as dependent on the fundamental sacrament of baptism, as a remembrance of it and to reactivate it." Since it takes time to become a Christian, the present practice of celebrating confirmation in middle to late adolescence brings out the gradual process of initiation. Confirmation "remembers" baptism because it is "by being confirmed that we can best embrace the baptism which has entered our lives" (p. 128). When celebrated after first eucharist, confirmation "remembers" and "confirms" both baptism and eucharist.

While this dialogue among liturgists, catechists, theologians and pastors goes on, persons young and old continue to be initiated into the church. In the concrete circumstances of parish life, theories take on odd-sized configurations. The old adage that nothing works so well in practice as a good theory may be true. But at the same time, practicing the faith precedes theologizing about it. Our current practice of initiation may be leading us into new and deeper understandings of the initiation sacraments. Our own experience at St. Elizabeth of Hungary parish in Acton, Massachusetts bears this out.

In 1977 after our parish decided to move confirmation from middle school to high school, we developed a process based on the RCIA. This catechumenal-style process followed the structure of pre-catechumenate, catechumenate, illumination and mystagogy. We worked to incorporate the vision and spirit of the RCIA through an emphasis on the role of the parish community, conversion and a "deschooling" of the initiation process. Over the past ten years this basic vision and direction has remained constant. We added and subtracted some things: materials, activities, certain expectations. But even after ten years we are just beginning. With this confirmation process and a parish catechumenate for adults, we still have a long way to go to make St. Elizabeth of Hungary a catechumenal parish. Without it, however, life at St. Elizabeth's would be quite different. If, as Henri Bourgeois suggests, the sacraments of initiation are meant both to "remember" and "reactivate" faith in the already initiated members, then this has had lasting effects for many.

Having read and listened to the discussions of liturgists and theologians, my own bias continues to be with the pastoral dimensions of the question. Our present policy of celebrating confirmation with adolescents draws on the insights of Thomas Marsh, Henri Bourgeois, Edward Miller, Kieran Sawyer, Thomas Zanzig and others. It should be noted, however, that each of them underlines the initiatory aspect of confirmation and its intimate relationship with baptism and eucharist. Hence the need for an RCIA-inspired preparation with a focus on formation.

There is a wonderful meditation on this and other basic cate-chumenal values in RCIA, 75. For adolescents, these values translate into enculturation: a response to adolescent points of view, to the need to bring Christian faith and adolescent lifestyle together.

Textbooks—even RCIA-inspired ones—do not work. They continue a classroom model foreign to a catechumenal process. Through listening and reflecting we have determined themes central to the information/formation process of Christian initia-tion. To develop these we have turned primarily to *Sharing the Christian Message,* Tom Zanzig's excellent high school material, choosing sessions on Jesus, church, sacraments, charity and jus-tice, life directions. This resource has brought a dynamic, living quality to our small and large group gatherings.

We work hard to place the lectionary in the center of prepara-tion for confirmation and to recommend it as a critical resource for an ongoing spirituality. Because eucharist continually initi-ates us more deeply into the church community throughout our lives, the lectionary offers a solid basis for day-to-day spirituality. In every lectionary session we attempt to shed light on how God's word and work lead to thanksgiving, eucharist.

Both sponsors and candidates receive *At Home with the Word* (Liturgy Training Publications, Chicago), an aid for reflection on the Sunday scripture readings. As resources we keep *God's Word Today* (Servant Publications, monthly), *Breaking Open the Word of God,* edited by Karen Hinman Powell and Joseph P. Sinwell (Paulist Press, 1986, 1987, 1988) and *Share the Word* (Paulist National Catholic Evangelization Association, monthly). These help catechists prepare for discussions on the lectionary. Spon-sors are encouraged to do the same when they meet individually with their candidates.

Catechists and sponsors form the core of confirmation min-istry. Each year we average about one hundred candidates for confirmation. The candidates are formed into groups of six to eight candidates with a catechist. These groups meet regularly for prayer, discussion, reflection—part of the formation/information process. Catechists, too, gather monthly for preparation, prayer and mutual support.

Each candidate chooses a sponsor at the beginning of the process. As in the adult catechumenate, this sponsor is perhaps the key person in the whole process. A sponsor who takes this ministry seriously can have a lasting effect on the candidate; in fact, a healthy and deep relationship that continues after the celebration of confirmation is common. To help sponsors appreciate the importance of this ministry we give each one a copy of *When a Teenager Chooses You* by Joseph Moore (St. Anthony Messenger Press) to read and reflect on. The sponsors meet together as a group several times during the entire process for encouragement, direction and prayer.

Since the entire process lasts about fifteen to sixteen months —January of one year to Eastertime of the next—the sponsors and the catechists, as well as the candidates, must be willing to make this commitment. It offers ample time for the candidates— and sponsors—to remember and reactivate their baptism and eucharist.

Throughout confirmation preparation, there are monthly sessions for all sponsors, candidates and catechists. With retreats, Christian service experiences, regular small group gatherings, Sunday evening dinners with the parish priests, and the relationship with sponsors, these monthly sessions provide the main formation structure for confirmation preparation.

This leads to Lent, the traditional enlightenment period for catechumens and other members of the parish community. We celebrate a presentation rite during mass on the First Sunday of Lent, reading the names of those to be confirmed, blessing them and asking parishioners to pray for them throughout the forty days. On the Second Sunday of Lent candidates and sponsors gather with the assembly for a rite of strengthening and healing. A celebration of faith—centered on the Creed—takes place halfway through Lent during evening prayer. We take care to keep these rites separate from the RCIA Lenten rites. We celebrate confirmation close to Easter, usually on Easter Saturday.

The Miami survey asked if there was continued involvement

after confirmation. Opinions were divided, with the majority (48%) noting a moderate increase. This followed on a 76% agreement that commitment increases when the age for confirmation is higher. These point to the importance of mystagogy for confirmation. If we expect all the newly-confirmed teenagers to join our youth ministry programs or continue some direct involvement in the parish beyond Sunday eucharist, we may be disappointed. We have no way of measuring the everyday ministry and commitment flowing from this process. Already confirmed teenagers make a significant contribution by speaking at confirmation sessions and leading retreats. They participate in some parish commissions and as eucharistic ministers, lectors and catechists. As with the adult catechumenate, the parish is continually challenged to clarify its own mission in the wider community, offering a vision of ministry in both church and world.

With the RCIA on the scene, confirmation must be different. We have tried to take this seriously by joining the vision of the catechumenate with that of confirmation developed in a living tradition. At the same time care must be taken not to confuse this confirmation preparation with the RCIA. While the RCIA may stand as a model for this vision, it nevertheless has a unique place in the parish's life.

Discussions about the meaning and place of confirmation continue, as well they should. Only through the dialogue of pastoral practice and theological/liturgical reflection will we arrive at an initiation practice that touches both the inner life of the church and the society of which that church is a part. Then our sacramental practice will be determined by the spirit and truth of Jesus' vision of God's reign.

Chapter 6

CONFIRMATION AT AGE SIXTEEN: MILWAUKEE'S STORY

Lynn Neu

Applause filled the room when Archbishop Weakland announced his confirmation decision to the diocesan Directors of Youth Ministry gathered in Milwaukee for the national CYO convention in 1981. Sixteen would now be the minimal age for celebrating confirmation in the Milwaukee archdiocese. These directors applauded because they knew that confirmation would enhance youth ministry. They also knew that youth ministry would enhance confirmation. More importantly, they could see how adolescent confirmation would draw young people into the life, mission and work of the church.

The applause was a long time in coming. Several years prior, the bishops of the world had been given the opportunity by Pope Paul VI to experiment with the age for confirmation (Rite of Confirmation, #11). In turn, the Episcopal Conference of the United States decided to allow individual bishops to determine the age for confirmation in their own diocese.

Weakland had begun the experiment in 1978 when, after broad consultation, he issued temporary guidelines for confirmation of adolescents. At that time, 250 of 315 respondents to the archbishop's proposed policy (150 of them priests, 110 DREs, 30 principals and teachers and 25 "others") agreed with him on setting a minimal age of 16 for celebration of the sacrament. It was also at that time that he established a committee of DREs, youth ministers, Catholic high school teachers, theologians, priests and parents to study the question further and to lend their expertise in writing the official guidelines which would replace the temporary ones. However, after his committee studied the question for more than two years, they offered him a different conclusion. They felt they could find no theology to support adolescent confirmation. After all that they had read, studied, and discussed, they proposed to the archbishop that the sacrament be celebrated with baptism in infancy or that baptism itself be delayed until young adulthood in order to preserve the original order of the sacraments of initiation.

Archbishop Weakland is not afraid of a challenging viewpoint. Grounded in an understanding of and an appreciation for the church's tradition and sacred scripture, as well as a sense of the faithful, he moves, sometimes boldly, in directions that seem to him to be most consistent with the Spirit of God for this day and age. His response to this committee, which had worked hard to come to a conclusion that seemed, at best, a compromise position, was that he knew of no theology that worked that was not based on the life experience of the people. He felt that neither option they proposed would jibe with that experience. While the committee felt strongly that none of the liturgical thelogians they studied seemed to support adolescent confirmation, Archbishop Weakland remained firm in his conviction that adolescent confirmation was the way to go at this time. His convictions stem from his sense that the developments of this sacrament throughout history cannot be negated. He is convinced that the twentieth century Holy Spirit has just as much power as the fourth century Holy Spirit. The developments that have occurred are not aberrations of the Spirit. The movement we experience, he feels, is guided by the Spirit and is responsive to the culture and time in which we live. While a return to the original order of the sacraments of initiation may preserve history, it may not be where the Spirit is leading.

It was clear at this meeting that new ground was being broken. There really was no precedent for celebrating confirmation in adolescence. While a case for infant or adult confirmation could be made, Weakland felt strongly that a case for adolescent confirmation could be made as well. Even though a truly mature commitment may not be possible until later, he felt that this time of preparation during adolescence would open the door to a maturing faith. It would initiate the process of lifelong faith development.

So, it was back to the drawing board for this committee. Their job now was to write the official guidelines for the confirmation of adolescents in the archdiocese of Milwaukee. One year later, in 1981, those guidelines were published.

The applause of the diocesan directors at the CYO convention seemed to pick up momentum in the years that followed. Many dioceses throughout the country and even some from abroad requested copies of Milwaukee's guidelines. Publishers began to pick up on this new movement. At first there were just two resources available for preparing adolescents for confirmation; now there are at least a dozen.

In 1983, the diocese of Youngstown, Ohio conducted a survey to determine just how strong this trend was. One hundred and thirty-one or 79% of the dioceses in the country responded to their survey. Of those who responded, 51% were celebrating confirmation during the high school years. In 1986, the archdiocese of New Orleans conducted another survey in preparation for their archdiocesan synod. One hundred and six or 68% of the dioceses responded. Of those, 60% said that their diocese "normally celebrates confirmation during the high school years, grades 9–12." On an average, they reported a 7.3 rating regarding satisfaction with this practice (on a 10 point scale with 10 standing for "great satisfaction"); 26% said their diocese was "presently considering a change in policy that would make confirmation of Catholic youth during high school years the norm."

So what has been the impact of these confirmation policies on the faith life of young people, their parents, their parishes, and the church at large? What story is unfolding regarding this pastoral practice that has gained such widespread support? The Youth Ministry Office of the Archdiocese of Milwaukee has been tracking this story both formally and informally for over ten years. They have been listening to parents, teens, confirmation coordinators, retreat directors, pastors and their bishops. The stories they hear often unfold with great enthusiasm. While there are concerns related to this component or that of confirmation programs, overwhelmingly those concerned with adolescent confirmation want to tell what has been so good about preparing teens for confirmation.

They are excited about the way young people are beginning to establish a parish identity. Through confirmation, the parish invites teens in a new way to "come and see" what church is all about. It takes their maturity seriously. It reaches out to them and says "you are important to this parish—not just for what you will bring to it in the future, but for the gifts you share now. We want you to be a part of us. We commit ourselves and our resources to help you to grow in your faith."

Parish religious education programs, which had been so weak in earlier years, are now seen as regaining or finding their dynamism. There is a focus to the effort. Parents have been supportive, primarily because a sacrament is involved, but nonetheless they are supportive—something that wasn't as true of "plain ole' religious ed. classes." True, this has not been the case for all parishes or all parents, but a new story of teens and their faith development is emerging.

Young people are being reconnected to their parishes and many of them are liking it! Of course, there are those youth who resist or those who are not ready. That's simply part of growing through adolescence. It's young people's job to rebel, to question, to resist. They are in the process of moving from "affiliative faith," where they believe basically what their parents believe, to "searching faith," where they ask the questions that will allow them to own the faith for themselves. Parish identity at a time like this is not easy to establish. However, what can be established is a "holding environment," a space where the adult community shows its concern about young people's questions, takes them seriously and walks with them.

In his May 24, 1990 "Herald of Hope" column in Milwaukee's *Catholic Herald,* Archbishop Weakland reflected on a year in which he had been "especially edified by the young people being confirmed. . . . Most of all," he said, "I come away from this season of the year after the many confirmations with a sense of hope. I know that many will not persevere, that they will drop off and not continue to come regularly to Mass and the sacraments; but I know that the good experience will always be there as a memory and be tugging at them to return to God and church." Parish identity has been established. It has become a part of the religious imagery that teens will carry with them for the rest of their lives. Hopefully, this imagery of a caring parish will "hold" them through their searching years and "carry" them into adult participation in the church.

Young people who reflected on Milwaukee's confirmation practice found that it was not only parish identity that was at stake here. It went much deeper to questions of personal identity. They pointed out how adolescents are required to make decisions about every other facet of their lives during their high school years. College choices, career decisions, dating and relationship patterns, morality issues, lifestyle questions—all issues related to identity, all requiring their attention. Why, they asked, would a decision regarding their faith development be left out of the mix of all the other important decisions they were making? And couldn't this become for them a rich resource for the other decisions they faced? They talked about the many questions they have about their Catholic faith and felt that their confirmation program was a great help to them in dealing with their questions. They perceived the church as taking them seriously and assisting them in finding answers to their questions.

As parishes witness growth in the personal and communal identity of teens, they recognize another phenomenon occurring simultaneously. They see growth in the community as well. The community is challenged in new ways to "be" something for its youth. As adult role models emerge to share their faith journey with teens, the parish is energized and rejuvenated. Adults recognize anew their responsibilities to pass on their heritage to the next generation. They have to look closely at their own faith response. Is this a community of faith so strong in its convictions and practice of the way of Jesus that young people are being drawn to participate? Or is it simply making demands on its young people to fulfill a series of requirements that can win them the prize of membership in the church? Where the former occurs, young people's resistance to a large extent has melted away and they enter into the process as explorers of the faith. Where the latter occurs, they often drag along and fulfill what is required more because their parents demand it than because they see it as a resource to them for their journey in faith.

Parishes that involve themselves in the faith journey of teens often find themselves beneficiaries of the gifts of their young people. They are refreshed by the teens' spontaneity, generosity, vulnerability and growing faith. The involvement of teens in the different parish ministries as well as their service endeavors gives many parishioners a sense of hope for the future. They can see that something is being built here. The community will go on after them. They are also challenged by the unabashed questions young people ask. They are forced to rethink positions which they'd accepted long ago and which they hadn't had to explain to anyone for years. This brings greater clarity to their own thought and greater appreciation for the complexity of the issues. As adolescent confirmation candidates grow in faith, so too the adults deepen in their faith understandings.

Another positive aspect in adolescent confirmation has been the involvement of young people in service to others. While confirmation coordinators have struggled with a "project" mentality vs. a "gospel response" mentality regarding this component, the experience generally has been a very rich one for the teens. Many of them discover a sense of self-esteem as they shift the focus from self-centered concerns to the much more basic needs of those they help. They gain a new perspective on their own problems and they draw strength from the bonds they form with their new friends. Many have had to deal with their prejudices as they serve the poor. It is more difficult to blame friends than it is the faceless poor for their situation. Some have even discovered career directions through their involvement in service projects. They never realized that they could be so good at relating to people in need, or that they could find so much satisfaction, or that they could learn so much about themselves, or even that these experiences could draw them closer to God.

The retreat, which is a requirement for confirmation preparation in the Milwaukee archdiocese, has been described as "an absolutely wonderful" experience for many teens and the "highlight" of confirmation preparation. Archbishop Weakland commented on this component in his May 24 column in the *Catholic Herald*. He said: "It is evident that the retreat is a high point in the preparation for Confirmation. At that point religion ceases to be a school or academic subject like all the others and becomes important to life. That moment is indeed a decisive one. From then on young persons seem to see that God is important to them and to their lives."

Many experienced confirmation coordinators have recognized the power of the retreat and have decided not to wait until the end of the preparation period to draw on this power. A retreat experience at the beginning of confirmation preparation helps build a sense of community among the teens and softens their hearts for what is to follow. A closing retreat experience celebrates the faith growth that has occurred and provides an environment in which young people can affirm (or not) their decision to be confirmed.

Another advantage of adolescent confirmation, which is somewhat of a by-product, is the involvement of young adults. Having been so moved by their own growth in faith through the confirmation process, many are eager to bring the next group along to see what they've seen, to be enriched as they were enriched. These young adults come back, sometimes even from college on weekends, to help "sponsor" their younger brothers and sisters in their journey of faith. They continue their own development as they become discussion leaders, retreat helpers, and companions in service projects. Mind you, these things do not happen everywhere. It takes a coordinator who recognizes the potential in these young adults and who invites their further participation. And usually it only happens in those communities where something essential happened to the confirmands in the first place. Those parishes caught in the rigidity of requirements seldom, if ever, experience this generativity of young adults.

The crowning and most important "success story" of all is the fact that through adolescent confirmation, many young people are committing themselves to a life of faith. They may not have the maturity of an older adult, but they are ready enough to say "yes" to their intent to continue to grow in their Catholic faith. Many confirmands talk about confirmation as a major life experience. Their confirmation coordinators see it as a rite of passage.

Perhaps as you have read through these wonderful stories of

how confirmation has positively effected the faith growth of adolescents, you have been saying to yourself, "Ah but that's only
half the story! This is a rather rosy picture she paints!" Yes, this is
a rosy picture. It is some of the best of what can and does happen
in adolescent confirmation programs. There are parishes which
probably would not identify with these positive experiences.
There are still parishes which run programs with untrained catechists, with minimal or lifeless requirements, with little to no
participation from the parents, priests, sponsors or community
and who thus achieve minimal results. And there are still teens
who complain of being too busy to fit confirmation into their
schedule, or who resent anything having to do with the institu-
tional church. And then, too, there are still parents who are
apathetic, alienated from the church or skeptical about post-Vatican II developments. Nonetheless, over time a new script continues to be written and the momentum of this movement
continues.

Cardinal Law of Boston and Archbishop Roach of Minne-
apolis and St. Paul have just recently (Spring 1990) established
policies to move confirmation into adolescence. In his May 14,
1990 letter to the priests and deacons of his archdiocese, Archbishop Roach commented on the difference a good confirmation
program makes. He stated, ". . . where preparation for the celebration of the sacrament includes an intensive and extensive program of catechesis and is directed to more mature young people,
we have witnessed many moments of grace and beauty and power-
ful transformation." In listening to the people of his archdiocese
he found that "there was a belief that, among the various difficult
challenges in formation for your people, your Confirmation programs are some of the clearest successes."

While the positive aspects of adolescent confirmation can be
demonstrated, it is important to pay attention to those problem
areas which still exist. Five major concerns continue to be articu-
lated by those closest to adolescent confirmation: the retreat requirement, the Catholic high school connection, the consistency
and content of confirmation programs, post-confirmation programs and adult education.

The Retreat: While the retreat often surfaces as perhaps the most positive experience of confirmation preparation, it has also been named as a genuine source of frustration and even alienation for some teens. Questions about what "counts" or whether confirmation will be denied without fulfillment of this requirement, or whose retreat is more important, the Catholic high school's or the parish's, seem to miss the point of why a retreat has been included as part of the candidate's preparation for confirmation. Much of the difficulty with the confirmation retreat seems to come from a legalistic interpretation of the requirement. Some confirmation coordinators become so rigid in handling the retreat requirement that it appears to be one last hoop for young people to jump through before the tightly held prize of confirmation can be awarded them.

Difficulty also arises from the fact that many parents have never experienced a retreat themselves and are unclear about its benefit. Given that most adults grew up in a different era with different emphases, there is little appreciation among many of them for community building and faith sharing activities. They become protective of their teen's busy schedule and ask that they be excused from such requirements.

Parents need help in understanding that over an extended period of time, away from schedules, tensions and a fast-paced life of activity, young people can get in touch with the deeper questions of life and find nourishment for their spiritual journey. In a retreat setting young people have an opportunity to *experience* what it means to be a member of a community. And as they open up to one another and the Lord, their prayer together and service to one another takes on new meaning. The interplay between the elements of catechesis—message, community, worship and service—happens best in a retreat experience. As the group gets to know one another better through group activities, the trust level grows and they become more willing to share their deeper questions, fears and dreams. Through quiet time and special prayer services they begin to see prayer as a source of strength. And as they spend the weekend together, needs arise and they are called to serve one another. They become a microcosm of the larger faith community.

Many parents will not understand this dynamic unless the

confirmation coordinator helps them to do so. Through parent information sessions, involvement of parents as group discussion leaders on retreats, witness talks by teens regarding the impact of their retreat as well as retreat opportunities for adults, parents will gain a better appreciation of the efficacy of retreats.

Catholic High Schools: The role of the Catholic high school in confirmation preparation is another one of those areas that requires a great deal of sensitivity. Parents are spending upward to $2,500 to send their sons and daughters to Catholic schools that emphasize strong religion programs, and yet, when it comes time for confirmation, they are told that high school religion classes are not enough. Their teens are expected now to attend confirmation preparation sessions at the parish as well. The Milwaukee Confirmation Guidelines point out that Catholic high school students are not expected to participate in all elements of the parish confirmation program, yet what is underemphasized is that somehow youth need to establish their identity as parish members. They not only belong to a school community, but they are also a part of a parish community. While their high school community experience may be rich and perhaps sometimes even more fulfilling to them than their parish experience, it is important for youth to begin identifying with their parish as it is here that they will hopefully live out a major aspect of their adult faith life. Personnel from both the parish and the Catholic high school need to focus their efforts on young people's active participation in parish life. Each needs to foster a sense of belonging to a eucharistic community that will outlast graduation from high school.

The confirmation coordinator's job in this regard is not an easy one. On the one hand he or she needs to help the Catholic high school students feel as if they belong to the confirmation group and yet on the other hand must be careful not to over-expect and thus encourage resentment and alienation. One way of getting beyond this dilemma is to invite Catholic high school students to assume leadership roles within the confirmation preparation program. Granted, not every Catholic high school student is a leader-type, but each should be recognized as already having had some background in the matters at hand. They should be encouraged—and should perhaps even see this as part of their responsibility—to share the gift of their Catholic education with others.

It would be beneficial to work *with* Catholic high school students to achieve a balance between school and parish programs. Cooperation is more likely if they've been given a chance for input and if their suggestions are taken seriously.

Catholic high school religion teachers can assist parish confirmation coordinators in their efforts by encouraging parish participation, keeping abreast of their students' involvement in confirmation preparation, celebrating confirmation with them and entering into dialogue with confirmation coordinators whenever possible.

Of utmost importance to both Catholic high school religion teachers and parish confirmation coordinators must be the faith growth of young people. Parish and school staffs need to see themselves as partners in an endeavor that leads youth to Christ.

Consistency and Content of Parish Confirmation Programs: Guidelines are *guidelines* and so there is no *set* way to do a confirmation preparation program in the Milwaukee archdiocese. Flexibility is required if the needs of the very different communities within the archdiocese are to be met. The parameters are simply that a candidate is to be prepared "according to the guidelines." Those guidelines indicate that the inclusion of the four elements of catechesis—message, community, worship and service—are essential elements of any catechetical program, including confirmation. It is suggested that a one-year program is feasible and that a three-year program is unlikely. Yet, one will find programs in the archdiocese that range in time required anywhere from a few months to three full years. Clarification is needed in the name given to what is done. While an entire parish high school catechetical program offers the background needed for confirmation, it must not be considered "confirmation preparation." This would make more of confirmation than is necessary or intended. To call everything done in the name of youth catechesis "confirmation" is to reinforce the image of the church as a sort of "sacramental filling station."

Many catechists fear that if confirmation preparation is limited to one year, young people will attend for just that one year.

Parents want their young people confirmed because they feel it's their parental duty and they will generally be supportive of whatever leads to confirmation. Perhaps as parents grow in their own understanding of faith development as more than "getting sacraments," they will be more supportive of their children's involvement in catechetical programs that go beyond sacramental preparation. In the meantime, it would be helpful to encourage participation at all levels—child through adult—and to talk about the years before confirmation as preliminaries or prerequisites.

Communication between parishes in geographical areas is extremely important. It should be clear to young people that even though the design of a program may differ, the requirements are basically the same from parish to parish.

While the guidelines are clear that confirmation programs need to include the elements of message, community, worship and service, and while many parishes have become adept in developing a multi-dimensional program along these lines, a problem that still exists is the lack of *quality* in the content that is offered. There are still parishes that provide only a randomly selected series of speakers or films to entertain the candidates. There is little intentionality in situations like this regarding what is taught.

The publication of *The Challenge of Adolescent Catechesis* by the National Federation for Catholic Youth Ministry (1986) has been helpful in naming the need for catechesis that is both *intentional* and *systematic*. As that document becomes more widely known and as the quality of catechists improves through the many training programs that are now available, the more the content of confirmation programs should improve.

Post-Confirmation Programs: While a great deal of effort goes into providing effective confirmation programs, very little follow-through is done with confirmands. This is a major lost opportunity. Just when young people have committed themselves to further growth, parishes back off and offer little or nothing to assist them in continuing their faith journey. For a number of years, this was somewhat understandable because of the lack of effective materials to use in working with this group. However, today there is no excuse. Materials are available. And young people are ripe for further growth. If the confirmation program has been effective, young people will generally be eager to continue exploring issues of faith as they continue their transition into young adulthood.

Post-confirmation programs are an opportunity to set up a pattern of lifelong learning. Confirmation is not an end point; rather, it is the beginning of the adult journey in faith. Post-confirmation programs are an effective way of enhancing what was begun in the confirmation program.

Adult Education: As the Confirmation Guidelines for the Archdiocese of Milwaukee were implemented, questions and comments like the following could be heard from a number of parents: "Why can't our kids be confirmed the way we were? Why all these requirements? What's all this community business anyway? Just give them the sacrament and they'll be strong enough to defend their faith. We never had to make a retreat or do service projects to be confirmed. . . ."

Many adults' understandings are still limited to the rote answers they learned from the Baltimore Catechism. Vatican II has had a significant impact on the church and yet many of our adults have been left behind with their childhood understandings of faith. As we seek to put young people in touch with their religious heritage, we must also keep our adults in tune with a growing, changing church. Times of sacramental preparation of children are often times of rediscovery of religious truths for parents. Catechists should be encouraged to use these "teachable moments" to broaden parents' and other adults' understanding of catechesis to include not only the teaching of the message, but also the building and living of faith community, participation in the prayer life of the church, and serving the needs of others.

While these major concerns continue to need attention, one can see that much progress has been made since 1981. Program quality has been strengthened and a greater number of qualified and experienced leaders now facilitate confirmation preparation programs. Teens are growing in their personal and communal identity within the Catholic Church. Parish communities are experiencing growth through the confirmation programs. Prayer and service are becoming integrated into teens' lives. Young adults are often eager to pass on what they experienced. Even though frustration and lack of understanding still exist, the value of the retreat has gained broader acceptance among parents and teens. More and more parishes are recognizing the need for and are providing more effective adult education for parents, sponsors and the parish at large. The context of total youth ministry is enhancing the effectiveness of confirmation, especially through its emphasis on relationships. And confirmation is enhancing youth ministry primarily because of the importance parents and the parish place on it.

Each of these results is important and good to hear. However, none can compare with the significant pastoral advantage that adolescent confirmation has afforded—that of the transformation of teens' lives and the deepening of their faith. Through their experience of confirmation, they have wrestled with questions of faith and have come to some resolution. They have decided to commit themselves (or to wait) to continue to develop as followers of Christ within the Catholic Church. Through their experience most have chosen to become a part of the community and to be involved in the life, mission and work of the church.

Applause by the diocesan directors was a fitting response to Archbishop Weakland's decision to move confirmation into adolescence. Perhaps it's an even more appropriate response now as we celebrate the many positive outcomes of such a move.

Chapter 7

A LOOK AT CONFIRMATION THROUGH "SPANISH" EYES

Theresa Viramontes-Gutierrez

In this article I would like to offer you some *practical* ideas for confirmation programs with the Hispanic community. I offer these ideas from my experience of four years as DRE at St. Gerard Majella in Culver City, California and currently as confirmation consultant for the Spanish-speaking community in the Los Angeles archdiocese. Hopefully, you will find here some reasons to reflect on how you minister to the Hispanics in your parish as they prepare for confirmation.

The confirmation preparation process in Los Angeles is one that invites high school-age youth from Catholic and public schools to come together to experience the Spirit of Christ in the faith-life of the community. They enter into a process of preparation adapted from the RCIA which calls the candidates to commitment, to ongoing conversion and to a sense of mission personally, and as community. For our Hispanic youth, at the heart of community is the family/extended family. The extended family embodies the most important values for Hispanics: their language, their culture and their faith. Family obligations have top priority. "La familia viene primero" ("The family comes first"). Unless we minister to our youth/family/extended family, our ministry will be for naught.

In *Evangelii Nuntiandi,* n. 71, Paul VI declared:

> The family, just like the church, must always be regarded as a center to which the gospel must be brought and from which it must be proclaimed. Therefore, in a family which is conscious

of this role all members of the family are evangelizers and are themselves evangelized."

If we are to effectively guide our youth through such a preparation process we must be *sensitive* to who they are and where they're coming from in the context of their family and relationships, and take this opportunity to minister to the family, and support its mission as the "domestic church." Therefore, the format of my presentation will invite us to reconsider our process for preparation for the sacrament of confirmation with Hispanic communities by taking a look through "Spanish" eyes at:

1. Who are our Hispanic youth/families?
2. Where are they at? What are the issues?
3. What is a practical response?

1. Who Are Our Hispanic Youth/Families?

How would you describe an Hispanic? There are many terms —Chicano, Latino, Mexicano, Mexican-American, Spanish-speaking, Central-American, etc.

Each and every term is inadequate—it leads others to believe we know what we're talking about, and the reality is that frequently we *don't!* For instance: (a) What generation are they? Did they just arrive from across the border or are they second or even third generation U.S.-born citizens? (b) What about their language? Do they speak English only, Spanish only, are they bilingual, or do they speak Spanglish? There is a difference. (c) Where are they in the process of assimilation? Are they very much into their particular culture, customs and traditions? Are they struggling between the family's culture vs. society's culture and how and where they fit in? Or have they altogether "assimilated" and cannot or maybe even *will not* identify with any cultural traditions, celebrations, etc.? (d) Where are they from? Mexico, and in search of better living conditions? Central America, and in search of political asylum and religious freedom? Or from South America and in search of economic relief? We cannot afford to guess

—there is great diversity in the United States: socially, culturally and economically.

One recent incident comes to mind—my daughter, Marisol Renee, age seven, had just started classes at a new school this last September. We parents were informed that the children would be tested for appropriate grouping in terms of competency in English reading and writing skills. The school, located in Santa Monica, is growing in numbers of Hispanic children enrolled, specifically Mexican, Spanish-speaking children. Out of curiosity, I asked Marisol Renee how many "Mexican" children were in her class. Her response was classic: "Mom, what do they look like?" I deserved that.

The bottom line here is that we need to get to know our Hispanic communities—they will vary from parish to parish. "Hispanic ministry" means *study, effort* and *time;* it means *insertion.* We must be willing to get in there and worship, celebrate and work together. It means not trying to change "their" ways to our "American" way, but rather trying to learn and understand more about the Hispanic faith-life and use these very rich cultural customs, celebrations and traditions as a means of enrichment for all in the teachings/traditions of the church.

A PERSONAL STORY

When I first began as DRE, I assumed that all Hispanic children would go through the same kind of educational process I went through—no matter what (I am second-generation Mexican-American). That meant all learning would be in English—after all, I wanted to help the children to "assimilate." I very quickly came to the realization that when it comes to teaching about something as personal as one's own faith, it would have to be taught in the language of the heart. That called for Spanish and Spanglish classes as well as English classes. In this way the children were affirmed and made to feel *special* and *loved* and *accepted* in terms of who they were as children of God and people of faith (very much family-rooted).

This personal approach to teaching is a must, and must continue throughout the formative years. Just because the youth at the high school level read and write and study in English does not mean they must gather to share their faith in English. For when it comes to sharing on who God is to me and my experience of God in my life, *that* is *personal* and will come from the heart and in whatever the language of the heart is. After all, decision making and ways of thinking for most Hispanics is a personal matter of the heart.

This is not to say that only Hispanics make decisions and think from the heart—the point is that Anglo-Saxon/English-speaking cultures seem to stress the practical and ethical sections of the human psyche/mind. Stressing the practical, they are given to action—for example, everything must be well-organized and cost and energy efficient to get the job well done; stressing the ethical, they are given to obeying—and a willingness to conform for the good of society. The Hispanic/Spanish-speaking cultures on the other hand seem to stress the theoretical and aesthetic sections of the human psyche/mind. Stressing the theoretical, they are given to contemplation, speculation, reasoning and the acquisition of knowledge. Stressing the aesthetic, they are given to expressions of emotions, feelings and sentiment, an appreciation of ceremony and symbolism rather than substance.

I recall hearing about a university study conducted with three women and their babies. There was an Anglo-American mother, a Mexican mother and a Mexican-American mother, each with her baby in the study. The study stipulated: Moms, coax your babies to crawl from point A to point B. If the baby reaches point B, reward the baby with a candy. If the baby does *not* reach point B, *no candy!* Simple.

The Anglo-American baby did not reach point B—"Sorry, hon, no candy—those are the rules!" The Mexican baby did not reach point B—in Spanish, the mom says: "You're just a baby, mija; what do you know about rules anyway? Here's your candy." The Mexican-American baby did not reach point B—the mother just stood there; she didn't know what to do. On the one hand, she understood the rules and felt she must comply; on the other hand, her heart kept saying: "She's just a baby"—and she was torn for being placed in such a predicament.

The above story has its implications on ministry. If we as church approach our Hispanic community with an inflexible and business-like approach, we will fail to meet the expectations of the Hispanics in terms of what community is all about and give the impression of a cold and impersonal community of people, and therefore not attract them. What does this say specifically to confirmation ministry? Let's not approach preparation for confirmation as a well-organized, efficient parish offering a "heady trip" for the candidate but rather as a *personal* parish inviting everyone (candidates, parents, sponsors, family, extended family and the community) on a "journey of the heart."

2. *Where Are They At? What Are the Issues?*

We must make a concerted effort to recognize and surface those issues/concerns that plague our Hispanic youth/families/communities; these most certainly affect the Christian community as a whole. Dialogue with our Hispanics about these issues/concerns at every opportunity will eventually inculcate a sense of community support, thus reinforcing that they are not alone in their struggles and that we are a community of love, caring, support and fellowship—a *personal* parish.

Through our many gatherings with Hispanics, let's address those very real concerns and issues that affect their families' lives: gangs, violence, substance abuse, sex, abortions, etc. How many times do we wonder why our parent meetings are so poorly attended? Could it be that our approach has been a "heady" one, way above the heads of our Hispanics' experience and not one that takes into account the "starting point" of those we're addressing?

What all is involved in their "starting point"? What about the pressure placed on our Hispanic families living in this American society? Advances in communication, technology, knowledge and science are happening so rapidly that we are suffering from informational overload—what is learned today is obsolete in a few years. From the Hispanic perspective, while struggling to educate themselves and their children, trying to integrate the best of their culture with the best of the American "culture" without losing their identity, they are constantly threatened with having to keep up with the advances made in society or otherwise risk staying behind and failing. Many times this means sacrificing who we are as a cultural people. This all leads to feelings of overload, stress, depression, anxiety and overall changes in lifestyles —a tremendous crisis for the Hispanic family structure so greatly respected and valued, and the support system therein.

Another issue/concern to consider as part of the "starting point" of the Hispanic is that of the American church. It is largely seen as an impersonal organization with universities, Catholic schools, bank accounts, resources, scholars, etc. The burning issue is: As church, do we *live* out the good news? Does the church address the immediate needs of immigrants for a sense of acceptance, of ministers who are truly adapted to their language, cultural and social background? The church's challenge is to become a *personal* parish that can reach out to the various Hispanic communities. An important statistic worth mentioning is one that I came across through our "informational society": In the last three years, more than 70,000 Hispanic babies were baptized— more than all of the babies baptized in the cities of New York, Washington and Chicago combined. Ironically, another statistic reflects that whereas 83% of Hispanics consider religion important, 88% are not active in the parish!

Another major concern/issue is that of the *family*. We see the family threatened by separation, divorce, single-parenting, multi-generational living arrangements, violence, alcohol/ drugs, stress, and lack of communication. Culturally, Hispanics hold in high esteem their values, traditions and deep feelings about faith. There is a love and respect for family, a wonderful sense of community, an appreciation to God for his gift of life, and a devotion to Mary as intercessor. Our secular society, however, does not respect these values.

Our youth, then, are growing up ever more confused—torn between their cultural environment and the society's culture. Whereas moral values were received from the family, the church and the nation, our youth now receive their moral values from music, media and science. To compound this, our youth are living through the beginning of a new decade—and the trends that will affect them over the next ten years—interdependence, environment, poverty, peace, etc. When we remember Maslow's theory on the hierarchy of needs, can we be surprised that our youth are suffering feelings of distress, anxiety, and depression?

Our youth are hungry for the good news. When our youth look for help, for support, and they turn to us, will we say "Go to the English youth group" or "Go to the Spanish youth group" or perhaps not even be able to respond to their unique needs at all? Our challenge is to rethink our approach and to begin to form small faith-sharing groups/communities that will help them to identify, to be affirmed, to feel support and to be strengthened spiritually. There is a great need for spirituality, for prayer and for an outpouring of the gifts of the Spirit. Preparation for confirmation is our opportunity to respond to this need. How? Let's go to scripture.

3. What Is a Practical Response?

As mentioned earlier, ministry with Hispanics means *insertion*. To be effective we must, as we often hear among our youth, *get down* with them (youth, families) and get to know them and their realities. We can read, theorize, but there is no substitute for going out and finding out what makes them who they are. We must be willing to open ourselves to them and to share. It's a two-way street; we're all in this together. Hispanics can sense immediately if we are talking to them, talking down to them, or even just talking for the sake of talking. In being open and sharing of ourselves, we are communicating a sincere, honest and personal approach.

At a time when Hispanics seem to be ready and thirsty for evangelization, small faith-sharing groups on biblical study should be offered. Bookstores can hardly keep up with demands for Catholic Spanish translations of the Bible. The meditation, reflection, dialogue and contemplation of the word is integrated into the daily life and is put into *action*, responding well to the needs and concerns of the Hispanic community.

In approaching confirmation through ministry to youth and their families, we are reaffirming those values so often thrown aside by our youth at a time when they are most needed—values of family, respect for life, faith, culture, and language.

We have in scripture a model, a paradigm for our process of preparation for the sacrament of confirmation. In Luke 24:13–35, we have the story of the two disciples on the road to Emmaus. On the Sunday of the resurrection, these disciples journey from Jerusalem to Emmaus distraught over all that has happened to Jesus. On their journey the two are sharing their stories—they have feelings of disappointment, depression, and confusion and many questions. Surely they must have felt like "running away." Jesus himself appears to the disciples, but something prevents them from recognizing him. Jesus asks what's going on, what's happening, why they are so upset. He asks these questions calmly, gently, inviting them to open up to him. The disciples, with disbelief and surprise, ask if he's the only visitor to Jerusalem who hasn't heard what's happened in the past few days. Jesus continues to ask questions, carefully—"What happened?" They pour their hearts out about all the happenings and their feelings of disappointment.

This experience along the journey can be referred to as the human experience or, in RCIA terms, the pre-catechumenate stage. It's the time for forming of small groups of youth, special gatherings with parents and/or sponsors. It's all about coming together to get to know one another through sharing of our *stories*—sharing on such things as why we're here, where we come from, where we are going, what's going on right now in my life, what I am running away from. This sharing of stories, team members as well as those on the journey, leads to some key *questions* being raised and addressed. Through sharing of stories and asking of questions, a *community* is built—a community of trust, so key in the Hispanic experience.

Key faith themes that could be presented to youth/families during this human experience would be *identity, images of God, Jesus, relationships, community, call to commitment.*

During this experience, or stage, we must be sensitive to the backgrounds of the youth. It may be necessary to separate boys from girls for the first meetings until they are more comfortable with the small group process. We may have to offer English, Spanish, and Spanglish group sessions as well. This would be the time to build on their trust and then perhaps invite them to regroup, if they so desire, at the beginning of the second experience/stage.

In the gospel story, Jesus begins to interpret scripture from Moses through all of the prophets. He does this with patience and sensitivity to their feelings, helping them come to recognize what has happened. The disciples listen and are moved to invite this "stranger" to their home. This second experience is the Christian experience or, in RCIA terms, the catechumenate stage. It is during this time that we share with our youth/families what the church has to say, what Jesus says in the gospels, what traditions say to our realities. As a trusting community, they are now open to hearing about the church and its *teachings*. They come to integrate the Christian experience with their own personal human experience which invites them to a commitment and conversion in their lives. This is celebrated as they enter into the third experience/stage.

Key faith themes to present to our youth/families during the Christian experience would be *morality and decision-making, communication, sexuality, Jesus and the gospel values, church, sacraments and scripture.* In presenting these themes, it is imperative that we do so with the cultural sensitivity required.

As the journey continues further, the disciples and the "stranger" sit at the table; in the breaking of the bread the disciples recognize Jesus and he disappears from their sight. At this point, the disciples have had a profound *faith experience* unlike any other. They are now at a point of ongoing conversion as they reflect and remember their times with Jesus. This is the third experience, the sacramental experience or, in RCIA terms, the purification and enlightenment stage. The disciples indeed have felt purified and enlightened in terms of their life experiences. It is at this third experience or stage that our youth/families will have come to feel a conversion—most importantly, an ongoing conversion through reflection on the cycle A gospels during

Lent, retreats, and special blessings and gatherings. They will come to *celebrate* as a community the sacrament of confirmation.

During this third experience we should look to celebrate as many experiences together as possible during the Lenten season —for example, special mini-retreats, days of prayer, reconciliation services, scrutinies at Sunday liturgies, stations of the cross, etc. These experiences will be those very special moments in their conversion process just before the celebration of confirmation.

The Emmaus story ends with the disciples returning to Jerusalem to share the good news. This is the fourth experience, the community experience or, in RCIA terms, the mystagogia stage. Our youth/families will also return—to their baptismal promises, to a fuller celebration of eucharist and a living out of eucharist through their witness to the parish community with the gifts of the Holy Spirit. They will now share the good news with a renewed sense of mission. They will become our future youth leaders and group facilitators. The beauty is that they will be the very leaders we so desperately need: pastoral leaders with the sensitivity and knowledge of the Hispanics' language and culture surfacing from our own parish community.

Implications

• Adapt the family approach to your confirmation preparation program. Design the program so as to affirm and develop family values and traditions.

• Of top priority is obtaining materials/resources sensitive to Hispanics. When resources/materials are scarce, as is the case frequently, bilingual team members should be encouraged to adapt the English-language materials to the reality of the parish's Hispanic community. This is an excellent means of building on resources that address concerns/issues of the Hispanic community in your particular parish. When possible, make up handouts that parents/sponsors can take home for further reading/reflection. Also, there may be parents/sponsors who cannot read and would appreciate taking something home for others to read to them.

• Invite Hispanics who are comfortable with their culture and who are aware of the many issues/needs of the Hispanic community to form a *personal* parish approach to the confirmation preparation process.

• Provide pertinent in-service for confirmation team members regarding Hispanic awareness.

• Form small faith-sharing groups at meetings with parents/sponsors that will encourage Hispanics to reflect on who they are, their life and faith experience.

• Use scripture, popular religiosity, traditions, contemporary concerns/issues that will challenge parents/sponsors to be of support for one another.

In summary, in order to reach out in the true Spirit of Jesus to our youth/families/communities, it means *journeying together as community.* It means sharing *stories,* asking *questions,* building a trusting *community,* opening up to our church's *teachings* with cultural consciousness, leading to an authentic *faith experience,* which is *celebrated* as community through the fulfillment of our *mission.*

RESOURCES

Deck, Allen, S.J. *The Second Wave: Hispanic Ministry and the Evangelization of Cultures.* Paulist Press, 1988.

———— "Proselytism and Hispanic Catholics: How Long Can We Cry Wolf?" from *America,* December 1988, Vol. 159, No. 18.

Fitzpatrick, Joseph P., S.J. *One Church Many Cultures.* Sheed & Ward, 1987.

McBride, Alfred, O.Praem. "The Emmaus Journey: A Model for Religious Education," from *Catechist,* October 1988.

Movilla, Secundino. *Catecumenado Juvenil de Confirmacion: Orientaciones Pastorales.* Centro Nacional Salesiano de Pastoral Juvenil, Madrid, 2a edicion, Enero 1981.

Ramirez, Bishop Ricardo. "Hispanic Spirituality," from *Social Thought,* Summer 1985, Vol. 9, No. 3.

The Hispanic Presence: Challenge and Commitment (A Pastoral Letter on Hispanic Ministry). U.S. Catholic Conference, December 1983.

III

Confirming Adolescents:
Alternatives

Chapter 8

BUILDING CHRISTIANS: TOWARD RECLAIMING A THEOLOGY OF CONFIRMATION— A PROTESTANT PERSPECTIVE

Gary Davis

Recently a member of my church was describing his early spiritual experience: "When I was a kid, I wasn't given a choice whether I wanted to go to church," he said. "My father made me go, whether I wanted to or not. He said I could make my own decision after I was confirmed. So, I went through the church's confirmation process. I made my confirmation, and became a member of the church. So then, my father said, 'Okay, you're an adult now, and as regards church, you can do whatever you want.' And so, I did what I wanted: I immediately dropped out and stopped going entirely."

As he told his story, the irony of it seemed lost on the teller, even now. What had he thought he had been doing, becoming confirmed? What had his father thought he was doing? "Becoming an adult" seemed to be one of the underlying assumptions. But becoming a member of the church was obviously involved with it in some way, too. And yet, this was how the young new member evidenced his commitment to membership—by immediately dropping out!

Needless to say, as ironic as this fellow's response to confirmation was, it is certainly not an uncommon one. Whether explicitly or not, "confirmation" is treated by many people as something akin to "graduation" from church. It is seen as the *ending* of something—a "career" in church school, perhaps—rather than as the beginning of a new kind of commitment; consequently, confirmation is normally only seen as that act which may allow a person to put the church behind him, rather than as the act which only fully initiates him into the full responsibility of church membership. Put another way, "adulthood" is seen as something which the person assumes as a *result* of confirmation, rather than as something which should be assumed before the confirmation vow is taken, so that a mature, responsible, "adult" decision as to whether one should be confirmed or not can be made.

Much of the confusion that our confirmands and their parents have about confirmation today can be traced to the fact that the church itself seems not too sure what confirmation is about anymore. Surely, children cannot be expected to understand what confirmation is about if their parents don't; and their parents cannot be expected to know if their spiritual leaders don't. It is admittedly a serious thing to accuse church leaders of having little understanding of the meaning and purpose of confirmation. However, most indications seem to be that this is the case. Little thought, time or energy seems to be devoted in the presentation of many confirmation programs (in those places where they are offered at all). The pattern that most churches obey in their confirmation program offerings only keep to many of the old patterns of confirmation that have always been offered. But the result of those old offerings often wasn't very successful; and the result of the new offerings thus often stay the same, too—confirmation is seen as "graduation."

Sadly, little thought about confirmation seems even to be paid by the religious educators on higher levels: those who write curricula and offer advice to denominations. This is manifest in the fact that the official confirmation curricula that are offered by denominations are often so poor. The writers of these curricula may be good, even talented.[1] And the curricula get sold to the churches because the adults in the local churches who choose such things (usually the clergy) can look them over and say, "Hey, this is good!" But the reason that they may be good to us adults is that they seem to be written more *for* us adults. There is little within them to appeal to today's adolescent, to make him or her feel "engaged." Present curricula, as updated as they may seem, are still only the offspring of the old catechism technique of training confirmands. That was a technique of catechesis developed several hundred years ago which flowed out of a definite theological understanding of the purpose and place of confirmation which happened also to be appropriate for its time. Our problem is that, having lost the theology and merely holding onto the technique, we have made our sacred relic the wrong thing. And with times having reshaped the generations we now try to introduce to the faith, we have seen the ugly results—kids will learn "that dumb confirmation stuff" as long as they feel they have to, but given their first chance, they bolt. They are not integrated into the faith community, and they drop away.

I would suggest that if we reclaimed a full sense of the theology of confirmation—the very same theology which at one time led to the development of catechisms for training—in following that theology in the circumstances posed by today, we would pursue a wholly different route of catechesis.

The Present Confusion Over Confirmation

That there is confusion in the local church over what confirmation is supposed to be should be no surprise; for there is also considerable confusion present among some of those who make efforts at writing on the subject. A number of "theories" and theologies as to the purpose of confirmation have been forwarded. Two of the most popular, which have a whole host of variations in the way that they may manifest themselves in practice, are:

1. Confirmation is simply the process that a young person is put through by which he or she can assume membership in the church, just like his or her elders. It is, if you will, an "assuming of church 'citizenship,'" where finally a young person can stand on an equal par with others in the church by virtue of growth in maturity and age.
2. Basically and most importantly, confirmation is a "rite of passage to adulthood," a process of initiation, not so much into a group, as into a new stage of life—much like the puberty rites of other cultures and religions, e.g. the Jewish bar or bas mitzvah.

Whether consciously or not, the practices of churches indicate that the first of these two popular theories is the preeminent model which most of them follow today. To be sure, it has been the preeminent model followed by churches for at least the last hundred years, since F.D. Maurice and others outlined a rationale for it in the late 1800s. At the base of this understanding is that an individual's Christian identity is something which is fully assumed as an infant in baptism. Being baptized, a person can never be anything less than Christian. Religious education is simply the helping of individuals to assume more of the responsibility of their identity. A person's Christianity is a part of his or her identity, something akin to one's national citizenship:

> A person is born an American citizen and nothing more is necessary to establish that fact. But there comes a time when the state decrees that the person is of sufficient age (a feeling, thinking individual conscious of feeling and thinking) to assume the rights and duties of citizenship. The confirmation rite is simple, involving registration to vote. The first communion comes when the persons cast their first votes in an election. Catechesis concerns bringing the individual to conscious understanding of all that citizenship means, and thus in schools across the nation children study the history of the nation, the governmental structures, and all else that seems pertinent to good citizenship.[2]

Under this model, in short, the confirmation process is seen essentially as a form of ecclesiastical enculturization: explain the workings of the faith and the church in which the individual is expected to participate. But the problem here is precisely *in* that expectation. *Will* the persons we are confirming participate, just because we are confirming them and expect them to? Everyone knows that our children themselves do not necessarily make their choices based on what we expect of them. It is the element of *commitment* on the part of the confirmands themselves that is missing in this understanding. And advocates of this model as much as admit that. For it is those who adhere to this model who believe in doing confirmation at young ages—right at puberty, if not before. The reason? Those who write of their reasonings are bold enough to say that it is so the young person can be "captured" into church membership at a ripe age before he or she enters into the critical and rebellious stage of adolescence.[3] (And yet, experience tells any of us who serve churches how miserably ineffective that "capturing" works on keeping kids involved!)

The idea of considering confirmation as "a rite of passage to adulthood" had become rather a popular one ever since the rise of modern anthropology. After all, confirmation has settled upon the practice of performing its rite at or around the age of puberty, paralleling the adult initiatory rites practiced by other cultures. As LaVerne Haas points out, confirmation can easily be seen to meet the four anthropological criteria which mark such cultural rites:

> First, both Confirmation and the primitive puberty rites are initiatory events. Second, both events mark an attainment of maturity or fulfillment. Third, both events signify a change from the natural to the cultural man. Fourth, both events perpetuate the spiritual life of the community.[4]

Along these lines, it has not been uncommon for many to conclude that Christian confirmation is simply something of a variation or an outgrowth of the Jewish bar mitzvah.

One of the most visible and vocal advocates of this model of confirmation as a "rite of initiation to adulthood" is one of our own UCC pastors, William O. Roberts of First Congregational Church in Middletown, Connecticut. Roberts' book on confirmation, entitled, *Initiation to Adulthood: An Ancient Rite of Passage in Contemporary Form,* was published by The Pilgrim Press in 1982, and with its publication his ideas have come to influence the thoughts of many regarding confirmation within my own denomination.

However, in many ways, this model suffers from the very same weaknesses as the previous one. For what the "rite of passage of adulthood" entails is as much of an understanding that the basic value to be forwarded here is more of an "en-culturization," rather than necessarily an "en-Christianization." The presupposition behind the very approach seems to be that, as a rite of passage to adulthood, such a rite is something that everyone must go through in some way at one time or another in his or her life; confirmation is merely offered as one means to it. Moreover, the presumption that advocates of this model appear to carry is that the culture into which one is being initiated/confirmed is a Christian culture, and simply by being introduced to its processes and values, one will also absorb a Christian identity. An intentional *commitment* to the Christian faith on the part of the individual is something which is not emphasized (and may not even be considered something which is necessary).

These presumptions and presuppositions can be seen evidencing themselves in the very learning schemes which Roberts suggests as a way of offering catechesis. For instance, one segment of his confirmation process has a focus on politics. His suggestion is that, in the course of it, catechists do such things as get their students involved in an election campaign, take them to a polling place to see how it operates, and then follow up by going to a candidate's victory party. The point of this civics lesson? To "get in touch with the mysterious ways by which our society functions."[5] (Similar sorts of exercises are also suggested in segments of Roberts' process for initiating confirmands into the "mysteries of urban life," or into different stages of the life-cycle, sexuality and sex roles.)

Such exercises are not bad in and of themselves, of course. Most assuredly, they can play quite a valuable part in young people's growth in understanding of their society. But what is it about these exercises which makes them particularly *Christian*? Doesn't confirmation have something to do with being Christian?

The trouble with seeing confirmation as being basically a "rite of passage to adulthood" is that, while confirmation (in the way we have come to practice it today) may happen to meet the cross-cultural marks of what anthropologists have judged make a "rite of passage," those marks are not the *point* of confirmation. The *point* comes in the content and substance of commitment which confirmation is meant to develop and convey. That confirmation is, if anything, only *incidentally* a "rite of passage of adulthood" for youth of today, rather than *essentially* that can be seen in the very origins of confirmation itself. Originally, confirmation was a rite that went hand-in-hand with baptism, which, in the early church, was normally only done to those who were *already* adults. And the subsequent likening of confirmation to the Jewish bar mitzvah is also without foundation: for the truth is that the ritual of the bar mitzvah itself actually *post*-dates confirmation, originating as it did no earlier than the fourteenth century.

Karl Barth commented:

> Those who accept infant baptism should not in any circumstances treat confirmation lightly. . . .
>
> The familiar modern interpretations of confirmation which expound it as simply the climax of ecclesiastical instruction, admission to the Lord's Supper, or a kind of dedication of Christian youth, obscure its content. What if even in confirmation (or whatever it is called), with all due deference to the reasons advanced for it, there is again no express desire or confession on the part of the supposedly Christian young person? In [infant] baptism, those who were christianized without their own will or knowledge were baptized with a view to the faith which they were expected to ratify later. Are they not set, then, in a position where they must later decide and declare responsibly that they are Christians in and of themselves?[6]

Neither the model of confirmation as "assuming of church 'citizenship,' " nor of confirmation as "initiation to adulthood," seems to take this viewpoint seriously. Neither of them does much of anything to inform us as to how the church needs to go about its catechetical mission—a mission which can be defined as "building Christians."

The model of confirmation which truly honors the theological tradition of what confirmation was originally meant to be might be described as confirmation as "conversion therapy." Unlike the previous models which treat confirmation as being largely a process of enculturation, the model of confirmation as "conversion therapy" presupposes that the true practice of Christianity is not dominant in our wider culture, that everyone is not,

confirmation as enculturation
confirmation as conversion

nor will necessarily *be* a Christian—unless, that is, one walks the way of the cross. Everyone by virtue of birthright is a citizen of the country; everyone will by virtue of years become an adult; however, not everyone automatically is or will become a Christian. Thus, the requirements for introducing someone to the faith must be different. The initiation is more demanding: the rites are not made relevant to the catechumen, as much as the catechumen is invited to make himself or herself relevant to the rites.

The flaw in the models of confirmation as either the "assuming of church 'citizenship' " or the "rite of passage to adulthood" is that they treat confirmation as being essentially just another kind of *social* rite—the kind of rite performed by a culture or a race to which one is born in which one is expected to carry on "the tradition." But Christians belong to no such culture or race. Unlike even our sister and brother Jews, for instance, Christians are "*made,* not born."[7]

And a survey of Christian history leaves us with a key insight. It was only as long as the church took its initiatory rites seriously that it thrived within a pagan world. When it began to lose a sense of the theology behind the rites, and started to consider them as being something other than an initiation into a new way of life— a life of discipleship—which demanded something of its adherents, it began to decline in the power of its witness and its influence upon souls. As Michael Dujarier, one of the foremost historians of the history of the catechumenate, observes:

> The golden age of the catechumenate lasted only as long as the Church demanded of the candidates a real conversion and a sincere decision to follow Christ before they could be admitted. Once this necessary requirement was relaxed, and the Church admitted to the catechumenate those whose conversion was nominal or nonexistent, the catechumenate entered its long period of decline. The decline of the catechumenate went hand-in-hand with a general weakening of the commitment and lifestyle characteristic of the early Church.[8]

To come to some understanding as to the proper theology behind confirmation—as well as to see how the original rites of confirmation came to what they are today—it is only proper to take a brief look at that history.

The Evolution of Confirmation: A Brief History

In the Christian scriptures and in the early church, there was no rite of confirmation per se. All there were then were rites of initiation. Although it must be said that in the earliest Christian communities even these were not uniform, typically they consisted of three elements, offered in immediate succession: a baptism in water, a laying on of hands, and an introduction to the eucharist. The first two actions—baptism and the laying on of hands—were meant to reflect two distinct aspects of the initiation rite: baptism was to signify the death of the individual to his past life, and the laying on of hands was to signify his blessedness of a new life in the Spirit. The latter act came to be considered an essential element of the initiation because, it was felt, whereas "repentance and baptism in water are necessary . . . it is the reception of the Spirit which is the decisive mark of the Christian."[9]

Indeed, while the exact structure of the initiation is unclear among the first Christians, at least this much is indisputable: in order to come to initiation, a minimal requirement was that one needed to manifest repentance and experience a true *metanoia* and conversion, a turning around of one's life. We can see this belief exhibiting itself in the Pentecost story of Acts 2. When the people of Jerusalem are convicted by Peter's preaching, their response is to ask, "What shall we do?" And Peter sets down the expectations: "Repent, and be baptized every one of you in the name of Jesus Christ for the forgiveness of your sins; and you shall receive the Holy Spirit. . . ." "And he testified with many words and exhorted them," the story continues, "saying, 'Save yourselves from this crooked generation.' " The end result is that we are in fact granted the picture of a people who show true repentance and metanoia: "And they devoted themselves to the apostles' teaching and fellowship, to the breaking of bread and the prayers. . . . And all who believed were together and had all things in common; and they sold their possessions and goods and distributed them to all, as any had need. . . ."[10]

While what was required for initiation in those earliest days was simply the faith and willingness to respond to the gospel kerygma,[11] the growth of the church led to the perceived need of requiring of newcomers to the faith more detailed and structured instruction. The end of this, however, was still to gain from prospective initiants a response of their own commitment. The very word that was adopted to characterize the instruction—"catechesis"—comes from a Greek word which means not merely "to learn" or "to acknowledge," but "to resound or echo," "to celebrate or imitate," or "to emulate another's words or deeds." In fact, the new instruction requirement was adopted as much to provide a trial period for newcomers as anything else—a prospect's total attachment to Christ would be indicated by his or her willingness to undergo a prolonged initiation period and accept definite articles of faith. "The early Church saw the convert's first burst of enthusiasm for what it was: a fragile reality that was apt to evaporate as quickly as it appeared. The new converts had to be taught, tested, and brought to maturity. The ultimate test for sincerity and authenticity was always moral conversion."[12]

The *Didache* hints at what an outline of pre-baptismal ethical instruction and requirements of Christian living for potential converts might be, c.100 C.E. As such, the *Didache* indicates that explicit expectations of initiants were present in the church community from very early days. Nevertheless, most catechesis refrained from strict codification until the establishment of formal catechetical schools around the end of the second century. The most famous of these was in Alexandria, founded by Pontaenus, who was then succeeded by the distinguished line of Clement and Origen. Within these schools, instruction for initiation lasted over an extended period of time, typically three years (following the pattern which Jesus was believed to have established, offering a three-year apprenticeship in his ministry to the disciples). And the instruction in these schools was not merely cognitive and cerebral, involving the learning of doctrines and facts; all catechumens had to prove by their actions that they were endeavoring to make Christ the Lord of their lives. The rationale for such training and preparation was plain:

> The people who were being led toward baptism were pagans who lacked the experience of "education in Christ," who lived in a polity that either placed a Christian life in extraordinary temptation or even (in the time of the State-Church) made it difficult to obtain an assurance about their motives—almost inevitably mixed.[13]

With the coming of the third century, distinctions started to be made in the elements of the initiatory rites—distinctions which would later lead to a separation of confirmation from baptism. Tertullian (c.160–c.225), Hippolytus (c.170–c.236), and Cyprian (d.258) all began to make special mention of the part of the rites involving the post-baptismal laying on of hands and anointing with the sign of the cross.

Distinctions aside, however, the requirements of those to be initiated remained as strict as ever. In his *Apostolic Tradition,* Hippolytus was detailed in spelling these requirements out:

1. At the entry to the catechumenate, candidates had to undergo a first examination. If their motives for wanting to become Christian were discovered to be adulterated or impure, they were immediately rejected. Each candidate had to have a sponsor who was already a member of the faith community, and the sponsors themselves were examined to determine the aptitude of their candidates. Specifically, the sponsors were asked whether their candidates had enough faith in order to hear and to respond to the word of God. If the candidate was in the employ of a Christian, his employer could also be examined. If, on the other hand, the candidate was discovered to hold a profession unbecoming to the Christian faith—as an actor, a charioteer, a soldier, an astrologer, or a magician, perhaps—he was required to give up that profession.

All this was because "it was at all times necessary for the Church to be assured that the candidate had sincerely embraced the Christian faith, and that he had renounced his former habits of thought, belief and behaviour, before it was possible to bestow upon him the privileges and responsibilities of baptism."[14]

If the candidate after this first examination was accepted as a catechumen, he or she then received a formal admonition to lead a moral life.

2. Upon admission, all candidates were put through a training period of three years, led by clerical or lay teachers.

3. At the end of the training, yet prior to baptism, the candidates were given yet another examination. Again, their sponsors were questioned, but this time as to how their candidates had behaved during their training period. The examination, significantly, was not only over what the candidates knew cognitively, but over how they had led their lives. Particularly, what the examiners were made to ask was whether these would-be Christians had exemplified lives of *service*. "Let their life be examined," Hippolytus wrote, "whether they lived piously while catechumens, whether 'they honored the widows,' whether they visited the sick, whether they have fulfilled every good work."[15]

4. Following a positive examination, the week prior to a candidate's initiation was characterized by an intensive period of prayer and fasting, during which exorcisms and prayers for them were said by the community every day.

5. After the initiation, the newly-baptized were given one further admonition, to impress upon them that their initiation had not marked the end of a process for them, but only a beginning: "And when these things have been accomplished, let each one be zealous to perform good works and to please God, living righteously, devoting himself to the Church, performing those things which he has learnt, advancing in the service of God."[16]

As for the rite of initiation itself, Hippolytus makes mention of a practice which will have great significance in later centuries, as confirmation gets separated from baptism. He informs us that the baptismal part of the rite can be performed by any presbyter; however, the laying on of hands can only be done by the bishop. The argument that was later given for this distinction between the administration of the two rites was that it was all due to the story contained in Acts 8, where it was left to the apostles Peter and John to go and confer the "anointing of the Holy Spirit" upon the people of Samaria, who had already been baptized by others.

Through these first centuries, Christianity was still an outlawed religion in the Roman empire. With the ascendancy of Constantine to the emperor's throne, everything changed. The church first became accepted, then officially established by the state. And in what seems to be a direct correlation to this official acceptance, the church grew to be more lax in its spiritual practices. This inevitably had its effect on the catechumenate, something which was openly recognized as early in the establishment of the church as at the Council of Nicaea in 325. Those at the council could see already that, apparently, many were being baptized and admitted to the church with little or no instruction. They therefore adopted this prescription: "It is proper that in the future, this no longer be done since time is necessary for the catechumen (in view of baptism)."[17]

Nevertheless, this instruction by the council seemed to have little effect, and the quality of the catechumenate continued its decline. Because it was now the case that people *had* to become Christian in order to hold certain jobs within the empire, many joined the catechumenate for less than the best of reasons. Moreover, many of these, joining only for the status it conferred, did not even stick around to gain the benefit of any training, for what the state also happened to do during this time was to encourage the church to adopt a different definition of what it meant to be a "Christian": whereas heretofore a "Christian" was only one who had officially *completed* the catechetical process and had been baptized, the state (not wanting to wait through a lengthy catechetical process to turn out people for its "Christianized" posts) got the church to redefine as "Christian" anyone who as much as had *entered* the catechumenate. The result of this was that, having once gotten their proper "Christian" credentials by signing up as catechumens, many then saw no real incentive either to be instructed or to get baptized—and they put off their baptisms indefinitely! Discouraged by what they saw happening, the bishops only compounded the problem by changing the rules for baptism further. Since there were so few "quality" converts presenting themselves for baptism anymore, the bishops decided to abbreviate the catechetical period, so that more would actually become baptized. With more and more less-than-quality catechumens being rushed to baptism, the catechumenate degenerated into a shadow of its former self.

No less a figure than Augustine bemoaned this state of affairs. By the time of his episcopacy in the fifth century, what had once been a catechetical training period of three years now was telescoped down to fit into the few weeks of Lent. Augustine complained that this time for personal formation to a supposedly whole new change of life was far too short—but even he had not the power to change it.

It is around this very time of the decline of the catechumenate that the first explicit theology of confirmation was offered. Around the year 350, Cyril of Jerusalem wrote the "24 Catecheses." In these he provided the basic understanding that confirmation was something of a "cap" to baptism. Baptism, he said, linked an individual to the crucified and risen Christ; following up on that, the laying on of hands of confirmation was that rite which then conferred upon the individual a share in Christ's messianic priesthood. Clearly, with such an understanding, Cyril's theology was still that this initiation was one into a new way of life, one in which, as a "priest" after the likeness of Christ, one was to mediate, offer oneself, and serve.

With the fall of Rome came that vast period now known as the middle ages. The middle ages are often thought of as a time of a great flowering in the Christian faith, when the church rose to a height of power and influence which has been unsurpassed. Ironically, though, this was also the period during which formal training for Christian initiation almost totally disintegrated, to the point that the liturgy and even basic Christian beliefs became practically incomprehensible to the great mass of people.

Naturally, throughout this period there were those who saw what was happening and valiantly cried out for reform in the catechetical process. To read their words today, however, not only tells us that they had a sensitivity to the problem, but, by the minimal actions that they were seeking for reform, exactly into what state the process had fallen. It appears that hordes were being initiated into the faith without any training in Christianity at all!

- Pope Siricius (385), Pope Leo (447), the Council of Agde (506), and Pope Gregory II (c.700) all insisted that baptisms be done only on Easter and Pentecost, in the hopes that, by limiting them only to these two days, proper schedules could be established for some proper catechesis to be done.
- Martin of Braga got the Council of Braga (572) to adopt a measure which required at least a three week period of preparation before baptism, so that candidates could at least be instructed in the creed.
- Boniface, missionary to the German peoples, insisted on instructing converts a minimum of two months.
- Alcuin reacted to the mass baptisms that Charlemagne was requiring by insisting that these initiates have a catechetical preparation of between seven and forty days.

In every case, though, it was ultimately a losing battle. It was a missionary period, and conversions were sought more for their quantity than for their quality.

It was also during this time that the Christian rites of initiation became divorced from one another, and confirmation arose as a rite separate from baptism. The reason for the divorce was a practical one: the theology to justify the divorce was only developed later, long after the deed was done.

There are two factors which, taken together, led to the separation of baptism and confirmation. The first was the rise of infant baptism as a nearly universal custom. The reason for this was twofold: the acceptance of Augustine's doctrine of original sin advocated a baptism that took place as soon as possible after birth, and, with the establishment of a society so dominated by the church that everyone was outrightly *expected* to be Christian, giving them that formal identity at birth seemed to be just as appropriate a time as any.

The second factor which led to the separation of confirmation from baptism was the belief (outlined by Hippolytus earlier) that, while baptisms could be performed by the local priest, confirmation was solely the prerogative of the bishop. Originally, an insistence was made that the post-baptismal rites performed by the bishop be done as soon as possible after the baptism; the bishop was expected to make his rounds to the parish within the next week or month. However, as the church and concurrent demands upon a bishop's time and energies grew, the accessibility of the bishop became problematic. In large dioceses, bishops could only visit people infrequently because of the great distances to travel. Moreover, some bishops were habitually poor visitors, and by the time of Charlemagne they had been given many state duties to perform in addition to their ecclesiastical functions. Consequently, extensive delays between an individual's baptism and confirmation became commonplace, so that they even lasted into years. While the prerogative of the bishop to administer the post-baptismal rites did not presuppose that baptism and confirmation be two separate rites, such practical circumstances in fact made this the case.

Parents themselves had some complicity in widening the gap of years between baptism and confirmation, too. For even when they had the chance at a bishop's infrequent visit, many were not diligent in immediately presenting their children for confirmation.

> This was to cause Archbishop Peckham at the Council of Lambeth in 1281 to complain of the damnable negligence of confirmation, to obviate which he ordered that none be admitted to the sacrament of the Lord's body and blood, save if in danger of death, unless he had been confirmed, or reasonably prevented from receiving confirmation. The Diocesan Synod of Exeter, six years later, enacted a canon that any parent which did not present her child for confirmation within three years of his birth should be made to fast on bread and water every Friday until she did so.[18]

The separations in time between the administration of baptism and confirmation grew even greater as the decades and centuries passed—until finally the norm for the age of confirmation settled on adolescence. In fact, in other parts of Christendom, official decisions were made to set confirmation at that age even before the aforementioned meeting of the Synod of Exeter. The Fourth Lateran Council in 1215 approved the growing custom of postponing both first communion and confirmation to the "age of reason" (usually thought of as occurring between one's seventh and twelfth year, although it could be as old as fourteen or fifteen).

Incidentally, it was this same Fourth Lateran Council that officially defined the seven sacraments of the church, and confirmation was made one of them. With this designation, the divorce of confirmation from baptism was given its formal sanction. No longer was it recognized as merely being only the second part of the same initiation rite. By this time in the thirteenth century, of course, much of the memory had been lost that the only reason the two had become separated in the first place was because of practical circumstances, and justification for the divorce had been given adequate theological grounds. Those theological grounds came through what are today known as the "False Decretals," which, interestingly enough, have since been universally judged by modern scholarship to be forgeries. The False Decretals, attributed to a fictitious fourth century pope named Melchiadus (they were actually first published around 850), outlined how confirmation's purpose was something *other* than baptism—it was to bestow "an increase of grace" upon the individual over and above what baptism had any power of bestowing.[19]

Correspondingly, with these developments, the catechesis offered to someone in preparation for initiation had to take its own different turn. With baptism administered in infancy, training had to come (if it came at all) after the baptism had taken place. Thus, it came now to be the prelude to confirmation. Given the nature of medieval society, it was a style of catechesis which made a certain amount of sense. For with the church, its power, practices, and tenets, permeating almost everything within the society at the time, every person (unless declared specifically otherwise) could be presumed to be a Christian. A person really could be baptized at birth and, in a sense, pick up the basics of Christianity by osmosis as he or she just went about living life.

Not that "osmosis," in and of itself, was the explicitly recommended form of training. True, there were no formal training classes established and run by the church during this time. But expectations were upon parents to act as catechists for their children. In particular, parents were entrusted with teaching their baptized children as they grew the basic elements of the Lord's Prayer, the Creed, and (in the late middle ages) the Hail Mary. Again, given the nature of medieval society, it was not an inadequate system for training. For the domestic Christian education that a child received would inevitably have been reinforced by the other elements of the Christian life that he or she would have been exposed to—regular attendance at the liturgy, for example, or the sacrament of penance (always a strong means of moral instruction), all in addition to a community which itself carried strong Christian assumptions about life. Most assuredly, in the later middle ages,

> the [only] reasons for the feeling of many persons . . . (the reformers among them) that the system was inadequate probably had more to do with historical and social change than with the intrinsic inadequacies of the accommodations made in catechesis at the beginning of the medieval centuries.[20]

With the reformation came a change in the understanding of confirmation, but little change in the way of catechizing. The reformers—Luther, Melancthon, Calvin, Zwingli—rejected outright the notion that confirmation conveyed any special grace or bestowal of the Holy Spirit, as they feared that this idea detracted from the importance of baptism. So intensely were they opposed to the idea that even the use of the word "confirmation" came to be construed for many years afterward by their followers as a Romanizing offense. Nevertheless, while the *rite* of confirmation was abandoned, all of them saw the value of special instruction to bring individuals to a full commitment of faith. Luther stressed a need for instruction before the partaking of either sacrament, precisely because he held the sacraments in such high regard. While not willing to call it "confirmation" per se, Calvin advocated "a catechetical exercise, in which children or youths . . . deliver an account of their faith in the presence of the church."[21]

Knox also provided for no rite of confirmation, although he did require children to receive instruction and forbade them from the Lord's table until they could recite the Lord's Prayer, the Creed, and the ten commandments.

Thus, it is clear that from the beginning the reformers saw the inadequacy of bringing one to full initiation who did not have at least a rudimentary training in the faith—and to inform their people what those basic rudiments were, they developed the first catechisms. Luther published his in 1529; Calvin published one in 1545 (which he described as "a little treatise necessary for those who wish to receive the holy Supper of our Lord" and to know "the manner of questioning children to be received at the Supper"); Cranmer's Prayer Book of 1549 contained one of its own.

In the beginning, the responsibility of a child's primary catechesis using these catechisms as a basis was still thought by the reformers to be the parents' (and the godparents'). Calvin, in a letter to Knox, made it apparent that a child should not be baptized unless there was some evidence that he or she had parents or sponsors who were prepared to bring him or her up in the proper faith,

> for nothing is more preposterous than to insert into the body of Christ those for whom we have no hope that they will become his disciples. Whereby, if none of his relatives appear to pledge his faith to the church, and especially undertake the case of teaching the child, the act is mockery and the baptism is defiled.[22]

Among the Lutherans, it was up to the parents and godparents themselves to decide what the time might be when their child was ready for presentation, so no specific age for initiation was set. It was Luther's own conviction that

> Instruction in the church does not edify the adolescent, but testing in the home, explanation of the catechism, and testing in confession, these are worth much more.[23]

Again, it needs to be said that this practice of entrusting a child's basic catechesis to the home was not necessarily an ecclesiastical cop-out. As in the middle ages, it was entirely appropriate for its time. The basic threads which made up society all the way up to the industrial revolution came from the family unit. Catechetical instruction simply followed the same route as all basic education of the time: "it was the household, not the schoolroom, which for many citizens became the center of daily religious nurture."[24] Along these lines, not only were catechisms printed, but also a whole host of household manuals which admonished parents to lead their children in godly instruction, and show them the ways by which to grow in faith.

Not many years went by, though, when church leaders realized that parents needed to be held accountable to their responsibilities in some way if their job was ever going to be done. As a result, in 1537 in Geneva legal codes were formally adopted which dictated that parents must teach their children the prescribed rudiments of the faith and periodically bring them to be examined by the ministers of the church to see how well their instruction was going. In 1541 these regulations were tightened still further, to the point that parents were now required to bring their children to Sunday noon catechism classes. Parents who dared to neglect this responsibility were taken to task. The Lutheran Brandenburg Church Order of 1540, reacting to the fact that confirmation had become "an abuse and an empty ceremony," set up its own strict guidelines for those under its jurisdiction. Confirmation was declared to be the rite for those to come to

> who have been baptized [and have] come to an age when they know what they should believe and how to pray, and also know how they should lead a Christian life and behave honestly, as it is set out in the catechism.[25]

Bishops would now again do the examining and the confirming, and should a bishop find that candidates were inadequately prepared or knowledgable, he was to admonish their parents and leave them until an adequate catechesis could be done.

All of this was done because of the great belief that the reformers had that no one be initiated fully into the fellowship of the church without serious catechesis. Martin Bucer summarized the feelings of all of the reformers when he said:

> What a splendid thing it would be . . . if the only people admitted to the Lord's Table . . . were those who . . . were acknowledged as members of Christ because of the fruits of their life. . . . The rest should be kept among the catechumens until they will allow themselves to be instructed, and until the Lord directs them to receive fully the rebirth which he offered them in baptism and to make progress in their behaviour. By this means the lawful discipline and communion of Christ may be observed and the church of Christ may show its true face.[26]

Indeed, Bucer was consulted by Cranmer to critique Cranmer's Prayer Book of 1549, and in so doing Bucer got Anglican authorities to take confirmation requirements much more seriously than they had been doing. The 1549 Prayer Book contained this rubric:

> none hereafter shall be confirmed but such as can say in their mother tongue the articles of the faith, the Lord's Prayer and the Ten Commandments, and can also answer to such questions of [the] short catechism as the bishop (or such as he shall appoint) shall by his discretion oppose them in.[27]

Given his opportunity to comment on this, Bucer expressed his opinion that these requirements were much too lax. Anybody could memorize these elements of the faith, he said, without having any notion as to what they meant at all—or as Bucer himself put it, "it is evident that not a few children make a confession of this kind with no more understanding of the faith than some parrot uttering his Hallo."[28] Bucer's concern was that

> in every administration of the holy things of Christ care must be taken that some holy thing of the Lord is not thrown to the dogs, and that pearls of the kingdom of Christ are not scattered to the swine, and that the leaven of Satan is not knowingly mixed into the lump of Christ, and wolves are not put

among his sheep, and finally that there are not included among those that worship God in spirit and in truth those who honor God with their lips only but their heart is far from him.[29]

Bucer's point was that any catechesis preceding confirmation had to be full enough so that children not only could assent to the things of the faith, but could understand them—which would only be proved if the children could be led to the point where they evidenced an internalization of the Christian way:

> It is surely to be wished that children be not admitted to that public and solemn confession of faith and obedience to Christ (i.e. to confirmation) before they also have demonstrated by their lives and conduct their faith and their intention of living to God.[30]

Consequently, what Bucer imagined for catechesis was more than a hasty process. The leading of children to the faith would be long, involved and intense (something not unlike the catechumenate of the early church). He criticized the standard practice of the Anglicans that teaching of the catechism be done only "every sixth Sunday." This was clearly not sufficient, as "no art at all is more difficult than this art of living to God, since man is born lost to his sins," and "who could learn any art, however easy, if it were not taught him more often than the one day every sixth week?"[31] Weekly sessions with the catechism should be the absolute minimum, and Bucer gives a nod of approval to those churches which would do it even more frequently, as did some of his own German churches, which, he attested, taught the catechism on two days a week besides Sunday.

And apparently Bucer's critique of the 1549 Prayer Book had its effect—for in the subsequent edition of the Prayer Book, published in 1552, the rubric now stated that the catechism be taught on all Sundays and holy days before Evensong.[32]

Bucer's reforms notwithstanding, the trend of confirmation practice was to devolve from here, and it is within the next century or two that the traditions of confirmation which today influence most contemporary practice took on their form. On the one hand, a growing pietistic movement sought to put its own stamp on the understanding of confirmation; to the pietists, confirmation was seen as having largely a subjective value, understood as it was as being nothing much more than a renewal of the baptismal covenant. On the other hand, those nurtured by rationalistic tendencies reacted to this, and made confirmation essentially only a glorified rite of entrance into church membership. So practically did the rationalists understand the notion of confirmation that the age of the taking of the confirmation vow was shifted so that it coincided exactly with the age that an individual was made to assume his or her other rights as a citizen of "majority age." The result of this was that

> great stress was placed on the examination which was to show that the catechumen understood the meaning of the confession he was about to make to the world. . . . Sentimentalism was allowed free reign on the part of parents and friends. Because of the importance attributed to confirmation, totally unrelated acts were usually attached to the event by law (e.g. enforcement of school laws, eligibility to guild membership, voting and majority rights, and such church privileges as baptismal sponsorship and the privilege of marriage in the church). In short . . . confirmation became part of the social and national fabric.[33]

Yet other consequences flowed from this linking of confirmation with one's secular involvements. Since confirmation was now seen to be the education for one's assumption of adult responsibilities, it came to be associated with the time of one's conclusion of formal education in the world. Formal education typically ended for most people at the finish of elementary school, so that dictated that the age of confirmation be attached to the ages of thirteen or fourteen.

Moreover, the date for confirmation also became linked to the secular calendar. Spring graduation from school ordinarily came at Easter. Palm Sunday therefore became the popular day for confirming, so the confirmands could partake of their first

communion during Holy Week (this was especially critical tim-
ing, since, until recently, communion was celebrated in most
Protestant churches only four times a year).

All of these understandings then came to be transferred to
the United States with the waves of (primarily) Germanic immi-
gration in the nineteenth century. In the United States, the idea
that the catechesis which was to precede confirmation was nothing more than an assumption of "church citizenship" was bol-
stered by the ideas of such religious educators as F.D. Maurice
and Horace Bushnell. Bushnell's concept of religious education
was as "Christian nurture." According to this way of thinking, if
it wasn't proper to think of one in the society to have been born a
Christian, if that person was baptized as an infant, he or she was
certainly to be considered a Christian from the earliest age. The
task of catechesis, then, was simply to educate the child more in
his or her Christian responsibilities (his or her Christianity being
taken as a "given"). The explicit notion expressed by Bushnell
was that Christian education was to enable "the child to grow
into a Christian and never know himself as being otherwise."[34]

Contemporary catechesis and confirmation only appear to
be variations on this latter understanding and development—at
least, wherever confirmation is considered to lead either to an
"assumption of church 'citizenship,' " or to an "initiation to
adulthood." However, Dom Gregory Dix gives an enlightening
analysis as to the cause of the problems that so many churches are
experiencing in their understanding and attendant practice of
confirmation today. He argues that those who have downplayed
the place of confirmation as a fundamental part of the rite of
Christian initiation (and this would include even the reformers)
have been operating from a definition of confirmation which has
come to be proved is a bogus one—and it is precisely because of
that bogus understanding that the problems and the confusion
arise. Confirmation as it is practiced by most churches today,
both Protestant and Catholic, still seems to be structured upon
the assumptions that were laid out by the forgery, the hoax,
known as the False Decretals mentioned earlier. The False Decretals defined confirmation as a rite which bestowed an "increase
[or strengthening] of grace." And in almost all cases (until the

most recent reforms brought about by the scholarship of the liturgical renewal movement), those who have dealt with confirmation—both pro and con—have used this definition as the basis for their understanding. So the "pros" would have it: that which bestows an increase of grace must be a sacrament, and thereby should have enough objective validity to have power of its own; if the power is objectively God's to bestow through the rite, then who even needs to go through a period of instruction for that grace to be effective? (The Council of Trent in 1547 used exactly this argument, and determined the pattern for catechesis and confirmation for the Roman Catholic Church for the next four centuries. It defined confirmation as a sacrament whose grace was effective *ex opere operato,* i.e. not necessarily dependent on instruction.) On the "con" side of the issue (à la the reformers), their response was: If confirmation was only an *increase* of grace, what fundamental use was it? Nothing essentially different was given in confirmation than in baptism. So with that being the case, why even consider confirmation seriously? Do away with it, or, at most, treat it and its attendant catechesis perfunctorily. It may have some value as a "rite of passage" of some sort, but baptism is sufficient to bestow all of the grace one needs.[35]

The problem is that each of these positions is dialoguing with the wrong partner. It is dialoguing with the False Decretals, a statement which is now accepted as having no valid basis of authority. The contemporary church should rather be dialoguing with the early church, which established the pattern by which the rites of Christian initiation are to be understood. Neither of today's positions makes any acknowledgement that it recognizes the place that "baptism in the Spirit" had in the early church. Both positions effectively see confirmation as compartmentalized from baptism. And as Dix says,

> though Baptism and Confirmation are separable, they each become rather a different thing when they are thought of in separation. Something is lost from each, and also, perhaps, from between them.[36]

Karl Barth made no secret of his belief that the modern practice of the rites of Christian initiation needed to undergo some reform if they were to regain their integrity. He argued against infant baptism as a regular practice, because he said that a movement of faith on the part of the individual was necessary if one was to be initiated into a "faithful people." That being said, Barth acquiesced to the practice of infant baptism, because he held faith in a church which practiced it. Nevertheless, his acquiescence was not done without his strong insistence that there needed to be some act that occurred sometime within the course of a person's life where he or she actively ratified and acknowledged that faith into which he or she had been baptized. For "is not infant baptism only half a baptism?" he asked.[37] If the church was to persist in the baptizing of children before the age that they could make their own decision, Barth said, "infant baptism cries out for this kind of supplementation."[38]

And John Westerhoff picks up the theme. While incorporation into the church might come at God's initiative, he says,

> still, Christian initiation requires a responding person. For this reason the norm for Christian initiation is an adult catechumenate who knows something of the cost of discipleship and is willing to pay the price. Only if we maintain this norm will the church remain faithful in a secular, pluralistic world; only if we maintain this norm will the church be able to defend the baptism of children as a desirable exception for the children of faithful Christian parents within a faithful community.[39]

So the question comes to us: How might we reclaim a theology of confirmation for today?

Reclaiming the Meaning of Confirmation Today

Confirmation is one of the great rites of Christian initiation. Or rather, to put it more accurately, confirmation is really only a leg of the one *great* rite of Christian initiation. Confirmation is "part two" of the baptismal initiation, the "cap" to the baptismal sacrament. To say this is not so much to say that confirmation is a "completion" of baptism (such an understanding would diminish the importance of baptism) as it is to say that it is the "consummation" of baptism.[40] To neglect a serious treatment of confirmation, therefore, would in a very real way serve to devalue the true meaning of baptism.

As Leonel Mitchell points out,[41] put in its theological place, confirmation does *not* fulfill the anthropological definition of a "rite of passage." *Baptism* is the great Christian rite of passage. Confirmation is, instead, a "rite of 'intensification' "—it does not initiate an individual into a new way of being, but ratifies and renews the status conferred in baptism itself. The linkage between baptism and confirmation can further be described in this way:

> Both Baptism and Confirmation, regardless of their place in time, separate or conjoined, represent actions which are not so much those of beginning as they are those of intent. To view either or both merely as rites of reception or initiation is to deny the full sacramental nature of the action. In this as in other areas we tend to limit the inward and spiritual grace to the evidence of the outward and visible sign. It is true that Baptism represents a beginning, but it is also true that what is begun is far from completed at that moment. The intent, therefore, is not merely to begin, but to complete, to fulfill the promises and vows that are made, and what follows may rightly be considered to be of more significance that what has already been accomplished. . . . *Confirmation, by the same token, is more than a rite of passage. . . . It was never viewed as such in the early church, but seen rather as an occasion for the assurance of the strengthening of the Spirit to accomplish the work we as Christians are given to do.* [Emphasis mine.][42]

Seeing confirmation in this way—as an essential part of the great rite of Christian initiation—points to the manner in which it should be approached and treated by the church. Calling confirmation a rite of "initiation" makes us ask the question, "Initiation into *what?*" A biblically-based ecclesiology would provide the answer: an initiation into a special fellowship which, as the first letter of Peter describes (a "letter" which many scholars believe was in fact a baptismal sermon), is "a chosen race, a royal

priesthood, a holy nation, God's own people" (2:9)—a fellowship which, in honoring that identity, is not only that which is
filled with those who are ministered unto, but with those who are
to minister. In the full initiation rite, baptism is properly understood to be that which welcomes one into the Christian community, bestowing new life as one has died and risen in Christ, while
confirmation grants the spirit by which one is able to witness to
Christ, commissioned as part of Christ's priesthood, to the
world. The initiation thus is to be understood in no way as an end
"accomplishment," as if it is into a people which has somehow
finally "arrived" at its destination, but it is into a people whose
path is set by a continuing, ever more demanding journey—a
journey which is committed to further growth, to further service,
to further discipleship.[43]

Consequently, because confirmation is welcoming a person
into a whole new way of life, it is something which can only
properly be done with that person's full awareness, acknowledgement, and willing and conscious assent. In traditions where infant baptism is practiced, parents and sponsors speak for the
child, saying on the infant's behalf that he or she will be part of
the Christian faith into which he or she is being initiated. But
having someone else speak for an individual is not enough. The
day must come when the faith of the baptized person must finally
be "owned" by him or her, else the baptism itself hardly makes
any sense.[44] Confirmation

> is, as the word implies, a sealing, an acceptance of what has
> been offered, a challenge as well as grace, duty as well as de-
> sire, an intelligent commitment to all that is implied in such
> words as stewardship, evangelism, and mission, not to men-
> tion ministry. Confirmation is the action which represents the
> intent to be on the *other* side of Pentecost, the point at which
> the transformation occurs from being a disciple to becoming
> an apostle.[45]

Yet such an understanding of confirmation's purpose and
place within the baptismal mystery says something about the kind
of catechesis that must be necessary in order for confirmation to

take place. For if confirmation is about commitment to a way of life, how can any such commitment take place unless a person is fully informed about what that way of life may involve? Tertullian's famous quote that Christians are "made, not born" indicates that catechesis requires a full period of shaping the individual so that he or she may be made fully ready to receive the imprint of the Christian life upon him or her. As Alexander Schmemann remarks, catechesis must be

> not merely the communication of "religious knowledge," not training the human being to become a "good person," but the "edification"—the "building up" of a new member of the Body of Christ, a member of that new "chosen race" and "holy nation" whose mysterious life in this world began on the day of Pentecost.[46]

Indeed, the literal meaning of the word "catechesis" needs to be remembered: it is "to celebrate or imitate," or "to repeat another's words or deeds." Proper catechesis, then, would not only present an individual with the mantle of the Christian faith, but would prepare him or her actively to take it on (with all that that means); it would move beyond merely leading one to believe in God to enabling him or her to *love* God; it would prepare one at the time of confirmation itself to be able to make this vow of allegiance that John Chrysostom suggested for the initiation rite: "I enter your service, O Christ."[47]

Most of today's forms of pre-confirmation catechesis that have proved to be inadequate largely follow many of the same assumptions that shaped catechesis in the middle ages; and while those assumptions may have been appropriate to the world of medieval Europe, they hardly fit twentieth century America. In the early church, catechesis had to be done by the church itself, because no one else among an individual's other relationships (e.g. within the family, the school, etc.) could be presumed to be rooted deeply enough within the Christian tradition to provide an appropriate orientation and training. As the world moved in the "Christianized" middle ages, though, family units were themselves elements of the church. Therefore, transferring the responsibility for catechesis to the family only seemed natural, as one could expect one's family to be well-grounded in Christian belief and behavior. Today, however, both family units and family church commitments are breaking down. One cannot assume that a person is in a cohesive family unit which is also cohesively bound to the church. In many ways, the world in which Christians live today more accurately parallels the ancient, pagan world than the medieval "Christian" one. Hence, we cannot assume that a person any longer is going to receive primary catechesis from anyone outside of the church itself. The church must return to a model in which it as a body takes upon itself the primary responsibility for catechesis once again.

Recently, the most exciting work in the area of catechesis has been by the post-Vatican II Roman Catholic Church as part of the implementation of its Rite of Christian Initiation of Adults (RCIA). Hearkening back to early church practices, the Catholic Church has recognized the baptism and confirmation of adults as its prime initiation rite. What it has to suggest, however, may also be fruitfully adapted for use with adolescents of confirmation age.

The Catholics themselves are making some of these very modifications of the RCIA for those of confirmation age. But in the process, they have also made a noteworthy modification in the age of confirmation itself—a modification which we Protestants could also learn from. Confirmation used to be made in the Catholic faith at a very early age, around the seventh or eighth year. What has been realized is that that is an age much too young —for if confirmation is all about taking upon oneself a life of commitment to Christ, how could anyone reasonably make that commitment at such a young age? Yet what the Catholics have done in their new confirmation programs is to recognize that the age at which most Protestants did confirming—around the seventh or eighth grade—was also too young. This age for confirmation had been arrived at in the seventeenth and eighteenth centuries, after all, for no more substantive reason than that age thirteen or fourteen was that at which a child ended secular schooling. Modern studies in spiritual, psychological, and even physiological development have shown that middle-school youth are probably even worse disposed to make confirmation-like commitments than are younger children. Commitments such as they are being asked to make cannot be expected to be understood and taken and followed seriously at their age. The ability to think abstractly—a primary requisite for anyone who is to appreciate concepts such as "God" or "Those who would save their lives shall lose them"—has not developed except in the rare individual of their age. Neurological studies have even shown that the complex synapses in their brains which would help them ponder such things as ethics and idealism do not even form until age fifteen or sixteen. For these reasons, the new Catholic preparatory processes for confirmation—a lesson from which we can learn—are now reserved for those of middle- to late-adolescence.

The main thing that the RCIA reclaims (following the lead of the early church) is the understanding that catechesis is fundamentally a *process,* not a technique. It is thus not something which is comprised of mere *activity,* as it is that which seeks to foster commitment. In seeking to do this, it has a certain model to follow—a model which parallels that offered by the early church. But the model is a flexible one, because its assumptions end in the conclusion that no single "canned" program can be perfect for every community to use in every situation. The important thing is not to judge a confirmation program by whether it has been faithful to following a certain "recipe" of sessions; it should be judged on the basis of whether it has been faithful to Christ and to the catechumens who are a part of it. And this is measured by whether the program leads its catechumens to faith; it is judged by whether it results, finally, in *conversion.* For, as Westerhoff puts it, "without evangelization and conversion, [any Christian] nurture is inadequate."[48]

Indeed, any who have examined the catechetical/initiation process in the light of early church understanding have underscored this point time and again, that *conversion* is its very basis for being. Aidan Kavanagh refers to catechesis as "conversion therapy."[49] Summing up his study of the history of the catechumen-ate, Dujarier concludes:

> Catechesis is understood to be concerned with conversion in Christ and with how to live continuously in such a manner not only prior to but after initiation as well.[50]

The church itself has ever been identified as a "community of conversion."[51] And if our confirmation processes suffer from confusion, it is probably due to this great fact: that we have lost the sense that we are out to *convert* people, not merely to "relate" to them, or even to "instruct" them; that our purpose is to lead people to the place where they will make a fundamental turn in their lives, from self to Christ, where, as the confirmation service of the United Church of Christ itself says, they come to "live not for themselves, but for Christ and those whom Christ loves."[52]

But what can a catechetical process do to see that such conversion is fostered and accomplished? Clearly, sufficient time must be devoted to nuture and test a young person's spiritual understanding, beliefs, and journey. And in this category, most contemporary confirmation programs are much too brief. Catechesis in the early church in preparation for initiation lasted anywhere from two to three years—and this was when the catechumens had the sophistication of adults! How can we suppose to do adequate catechesis for conversion with teenagers in only a matter of weeks?

And so much time is required because the style of catechesis which is necessary to foster spiritual growth and understanding needs a lengthy amount of time to have its effect. If all we were teaching was *facts,* we might not need much time. With a little discipline, facts can be memorized and absorbed in little time at all. But developing spiritually is not about learning facts, as much as it is about *developing relationships*—developing relationships with God, with self, and with others. As Dujarier observes from his studies of the intentions of ancient catechesis, this period is not a time for cognitive learning about the Christian life, but rather a lived experience of that life. It is a time for *listening to the Word* of God which both forms and directs the candidate. It is a style of life where one is impregnated by the Word and tries to live according to it. [Emphasis his.][53]

To be sure, this is the weakness of most of the Christian nurture that we provide in the modern liberal Protestant tradition, whether that nurture is offered in confirmation classes, Sunday school, preaching, or worship—we focus a lot on "head-knowledge" about God, but do very little about cultivating "heart-knowledge" about God. We talk a lot *about* God, but do not do much in active dialogue *with* God. We focus on the cognitive level in addressing the things of the Spirit, but do little on the experiential level. Religion has been described as being comprised of two elements: "theology" and "spirituality." "Theology" deals with the facts and doctrines about God. "Spirituality" deals with the *experience* of God. Logically, spirituality must precede theology—one must have the experience first if one is ever going to have anything to explain. Our problem is that we have put the wrong horse first in pulling the cart. The Christian education we offer invariably gives people theology to the neglect of spirituality. And such is what cripples our confirmation catechesis. We give our catechumens facts and explanations about something that they might not even have experienced. What kind of sense is that going to make to them? In essence, we are giving them answers to questions they are likely not even asking.

Catechisms are a primary example of this, where, literally, answers are given to questions most teenagers are not even asking (to make up for that, catechisms tell the readers what questions they should be asking, too). Catechisms arose in an age when it may have been valid to presume that, because everyone was surrounded by Christian culture, they were immersed in religious experience. That is surely not a presumption we can make today. Yet even though presently available confirmation curricula do not follow strict catechism form, they still echo the old catechisms in offering theology instead of spirituality, telling the reader *about* God, rather than nurturing in them a way *to* God. No wonder, then, that confirmation is something which means little to today's confirmands. No wonder, after being confirmed, that so many of them drop out.

In what may sound paradoxical, if we are ever to reclaim a proper theology of confirmation, that theology would recognize the primacy of *spirituality,* the primacy of nurturing experience. Conversion is what we seek. And conversion is almost always rooted in an experience of grace, i.e. the feeling that, no matter what an individual has done, he or she knows that God still loves him or her. That being true, any effective confirmation process will be intent on helping catechumens, through their own experiences, to come to some direct knowledge of God's grace. For "genuine religious faith can only exist where it is rooted in personal experience and can find support in the way other people reveal their own religious experience."[54]

This is the lesson provided by the early church, and the lesson picked up by the RCIA. It is the lesson that *experience precedes understanding.* And the way this lesson was followed then (as the RCIA seeks to emulate it now) is that

> persons who desired to enter the church were immediately integrated into the fellowship of the community; further instruction took place within that fellowship, the mysteries were explained as soon as they were experienced, life was a reflection of that experience and that teaching. Worship, doctrine, and action were inextricably linked in the fellowship of the church, but it was worship that served as the key.[55]

So strongly did the early church believe that *experience* of Christ was of primary importance that such key elements of the Christian faith as the Lord's Prayer, the creed, and even the eucharist were not revealed to them until *after* their formal catechesis was over and they were officially initiated into the church. Catechesis was exclusively reserved for doing what was necessary to enable catechumens to model the Christian life.

Generally, this process of catechetical instruction involved four phases:

1. A period of inquiry and evangelization, during which an inquirer was engaged in informal dialogue and learning the essence of the faith. In order for him or her to pass on to the next stage, he or she had already to profess a faith in Jesus as Lord, and give evidence of beginning to lead a spiritual life.

2. The period of the catechumenate itself. An official "entrance rite" before the gathered community at liturgical assembly marked the beginning of this stage. The catechumenate

> was a time of instruction and spiritual direction, of grounding in Scripture, creeds and prayers. Evidence from the "lectures" or sermons in the early Church for this phase suggests that the goal was not to form theologians or "professors" but to ground catechumens practically in the disciplines, devotions, and affections of the Christian life. At the very heart of this phase was growth in prayer.[56]

3. The period of election. This also was recognized by a rite before the liturgical assembly. During this period candidates were now called "the elect." Occurring during Lent, it was a phase of more intensive preparation before their baptisms, which took place at the Easter vigil.

This preparatory period was also characterized by a series of "scrutinies" directed at the "elect." "Scrutiny" here, though, was not meant to be an examination of their knowledge; it was an examination of their *heart*. When their sponsors were finally examined as to the "elect's" worthiness for baptism, there were no questions at all about doctrinal issues. The sponsors were asked not what their candidates *knew*, but *how they lived*. Specifically, they were examined (to quote directly from Hippolytus in the third century) as to "whether 'they honored the widows,' whether they visited the sick, whether they [had] fulfilled every good work."[57]

> What is clear is that the examination was on the manner of life of the catechumens. No questions were asked concerning their understanding of Christian doctrine, or even of their

acceptance of Jesus Christ, although presumably some form
of rudimentary belief must have been responsible for their
initial approach to the church. . . . [T]he instruction which
they received was primarily in Christian living and was to
enable them to adopt what we would call a Christian lifestyle,
not to make them theologians.[58]

4. The period of mystagogia. This phase occured *after* initiation, between Easter and Pentecost. The newly-baptized were
now called "neophytes." This was a time of yet further deepening
in faith, which was accompanied by a fuller participation in sacramental experience and an exercise in ministry in and beyond the
congregation. The various rites of initiation were explained [note
the sequence here: first the rites were *experienced,* then *afterward*
they were explained, so that the neophytes might come to a fuller
subsequent experience of them. And, finally, they were intentionally directed to the moral requirements of a more authentic
Christian life.

In sum, the model provided by the early church identifies the
essential components of catechesis, all of which were approached
from an experiential understanding: grounding in scripture, liturgy, doctrine, prayer, and diakonia (service). The experiential
approach was enabled by the fact that the entire community of
the church was involved in the process every step of the way. The
most direct liaison that a candidate had with the community of
the faithful was through a sponsor, who interacted with the candidate regularly and provided him or her a model of what it
meant to live the Christian life. In addition, candidates were regularly presented before the liturgical assemblies to receive the
prayerful support of the entire congregation. Candidates were
also accompanied by their sponsors in involvements in all of the
regular activities of the church. "Hands-on" experience in the
Christian life came through the relationships with fellow believers that were formed in these very concrete ways.

And it is in this aspect that a further weakness is shown in
many of our present-day confirmation programs. Indeed, if much
of the experiencing of faith that early church catechumens received was through the relationships within and through the

Christian community that were fostered and built for them, then this may partially explain why our own confirmands may be deficient in much faith experience. It seems that a weakness of many adolescent catechetical programs—even good ones—is that, while a sharing and community sense may be developed among the group of catechumens themselves, a breakdown occurs in the integration of the catechumens into the larger community of faith. Hence, when the program is over and the class dissolves, there being no community of which the newly-confirmed feels he or she is any longer a part, he or she drifts away.

A reclaimed theology of confirmation would recognize that community involvement is an essential part of the process; it would acknowledge that ". . . Christian catechesis is always personal and individual, and, at the same time, social and communal."[59] It would have as a core understanding—and stress by word and practice this understanding to the catechumens—that the primary community of their training is not their class itself, but the church. For this is the community into which they shall be initiated, and through which their lives will find the support of fellow believers and servants as they go through life.

In short, what any renewed and proper theology of confirmation would do, if it is faithful to the roots and purposes of catechesis for initiation into the Christian church, is to center its approaches and culminate in

> the movement toward the love of God and the love of neighbor. Love, even the hard love of which Jesus and the gospel speak, is a fundamental shaping of the affections. It is a resting of the heart upon God, an enjoyment and prizing of the divine reality as the loving power which gives us life and calls us toward unity with it. The nurture of the love of God and neighbor, and the shaping of the gracious affections, require a steeping in prayer and a spirituality in which that devotion is celebrated.[60]

Conclusion—And Thoughts About Further Implications

Recalling Tertullian's observation that Christians are "made, not born," catechesis for Christian initiation should intentionally be concerned with "building Christians," and any theology of confirmation should reflect that understanding. For ". . . we [i.e. the church] exist to initiate [people] into the saving death-resurrection of Christ. We initiate in order to work with others to make the Kingdom happen."[61]

Any good theology, however, tends to raise as many new questions as it settles old ones. And the reclaiming of such a theology of confirmation would do just that. For instance, here are only a couple of the interesting issues that the church will have to deal with once it does take the theology of confirmation more seriously.

The main reason historically that confirmation became separated from baptism in the initiation rite is that while it was believed that any priest could perform baptisms, only the bishop could officiate at confirmation. Already the Catholic Church is redefining this rubric and designating as the primary minister of confirmation not the bishop, but the local priest. But what the Catholics are having to contend with as a consequent question, then, is: "If the priest can do confirmation and we don't have to wait for the appearance of the bishop anymore, then why keep baptism and confirmation separate at all?" Of course, proper initiation does require a response on the part of the person being initiated, an acknowledgement that the initiant "owns" the faith. So what this would mean is that if baptism and confirmation are to be reunited again, then confirmation shouldn't be lowered to baptism's age of infancy, but baptism should be raised to an age approaching adulthood (just like the norm set by the early church). And, in fact, the primary rite of initiation in the post-Vatican II Catholic Church, according to the rubrics, is the Rite of Christian Initiation of Adults. Infant baptism, while still practiced, is to be seen increasingly as an exception to the norm.

But what about us Protestants? We have never depended on a bishop to do our confirming, yet we keep the two halves of Christian initiation separate. Do they not also belong together for us? Is there anything theologically proper about keeping them apart? Perhaps Barth needs to be reconsidered: perhaps infant baptism deserves no longer to be the norm in a "post-Christian" culture.

Another issue which the church needs to consider seriously as it reclaims a good confirmation theology is this one raised by Urban Holmes:

> Initiation into anything more than the civil religion requires a discernible cultural community, which reinforces the values embodied in powerful symbols overtly proclaimed and lived in that community. It demands that we live principally in terms of that system. . . . If a group has any distinctive values it wishes to preserve and by which it is convinced every member must live, then it has to exist to itself as a community.[62]

What this is saying is that, if we are ever to expect Christians to be effectively "built" through the confirmation process, the community which seeks to build them must itself have unambiguously embodied the Christian identity and life. Confirmation catechesis has been called "conversion therapy." But in order for that therapy to be offered, the community itself has to manifest conversion. Simply put, "the renewal of the catechumenate cannot be accomplished without a profound renewal of all our Christian communities."[63]

What would it take for that to happen? Would the present state of our churches provide an adequate environment (a "critical mass" of the faithful) in order to engender conversion among the catechumens we teach? This is a question with which the whole church has to struggle. At this point, naturally, no one knows where such a struggle would lead, but perhaps it very well might be that a serious desire to reclaim a theology of confirmation could itself lead the church to consider the attendant issues so seriously that it would result not only in a renewal of confirmation itself, but in a revitalization of the entire community of faith.

NOTES

1. The UCC confirmation curriculum, *Confirming Our Faith* (New York: United Church Press, 1980), includes work by Walter

Bruggemann, Meredith Handspicker, Roger Shinn, Burton Throckmorton, and Barbara Brown Zikmund, for instance.

2. John E. Booty, "Since the Reformation: An Emphasis on the American Experience," in John W. Westerhoff III and O.C. Edwards, Jr. (eds.), *A Faithful Church: Issues in the History of Catechesis* (Wilton: Morehouse-Barlow Co., Inc., 1981) 279.

3. Cited in Richard C. Savin-Williams, "Age and Sex Differences in the Adolescent Image of Jesus," *Adolescence,* Vol. XII, No. 47 (Fall 1977) 353; this also seems to be the argument in Gordon Allport, *The Individual and His Religion* (New York: The Macmillan Company, 1951).

4. LaVerne Haas, *Personal Pentecost: The Meaning of Confirmation* (St. Meinrad: Abbey Press, 1973) 32.

5. William O. Roberts, Jr., *Initiation to Adulthood: An Ancient Rite of Passage in Contemporary Form* (New York: The Pilgrim Press, 1982) 135.

6. Karl Barth, *Church Dogmatics IV/4 (fragment)* (Edinburgh: T & T Clark, 1969) 188.

7. A phrase originally coined by Tertullian, c.160–c.225 C.E.

8. Michael Dujarier, *The Rites of Christian Initiation: Historical and Pastoral Reflections* (New York: Sadlier, 1979) 24–25.

9. Cheslyn Jones, Geoffrey Wainwright, Edward Yarnold, S.J., *The Study of Liturgy* (New York: Oxford University Press, 1978).

10. Acts 2:37–45.

11. See, in addition, Acts 21:41 and 8:26–40.

12. Christiane Brusselmans, "Introduction," in Michael Dujarier, *A History of the Catechumenate: The First Six Centuries* (New York, Chicago & Los Angeles: Sadlier, 1979) 6.

13. Alois Stenzel, S.J., "Temporal and Supra-Temporal in the History of the Catechumenate and Baptism," in Johannes Wagner (ed.), *Adult Baptism and the Catechumenate* (New York: Paulist Press, 1967) 33–34.

14. E.C. Whitaker, *The Baptismal Liturgy* (London: SPCK, 1981) 30.

15. Quoted in Dujarier, *History of the Catechumenate, op. cit.* 52.

16. Quoted in *ibid.* 54.

17. Quoted in *ibid.* 69.

18. J.D.C. Fisher and E.J. Yarnold, S.J., "Initiation in the West from about A.D. 500 to the Reformation," in Jones, *et al., op. cit.* 115.

19. Haas, *op. cit.* 26.

20. Milton McC. Gatch, "Basic Christian Education from the De-

cline of Catechesis to the Rise of Catechisms," in Westerhoff & Edwards, *op. cit.* 89.

21. Quoted in J.D.C. Fisher, *Christian Initiation: The Reformation Period,* Alcuin Club Collections No. 51 (London: SPCK, 1970) 258.

22. Quoted in William P. Haugaard, "The Continental Reformation of the 16th Century," in Westerhoff & Edwards, *op. cit.* 134.

23. Quoted in *ibid.* 133.

24. Frederica Harris Thompsett, "Godly Instruction in Reformation England: The Challenge of Religious Education in the Tudor Commonwealth," in Westerhoff & Edwards, *op. cit.* 196.

25. Quoted in Fisher, *op. cit.* 182–184.

26. Quoted in Haugaard, *op. cit.* 164.

27. Quoted in Fisher, *op. cit.* 236–237.

28. *Ibid.* 246.

29. *Ibid.*

30. *Ibid.*

31. *Ibid.* 248–249.

32. *Ibid.* 252.

33. W. Kent Gilbert (ed.), *Confirmation and Education* (Yearbooks in Christian Education, Vol. I) (Philadelphia: Fortress Press, 1969) 189.

34. Quoted in Booty, *op. cit.* 274. Booty gives an exceptional survey of catechesis during this period.

35. Dom Gregory Dix, *The Theology of Confirmation in Relation to Baptism* (Westminster: Dacre Press, 1946) 29ff.

36. *Ibid.* 38.

37. Barth, *op. cit.* 188.

38. *Ibid.*

39. Westerhoff & Edwards, *op. cit.* 310.

40. For an outline as to how this intention can be inferred from a study of the *missa* of early church baptismal synaxes, see Aidan Kavanagh, "Confirmation: A Suggestion from Structure," *Worship,* Vol. 58, No. 5 (September 1984) 394.

41. Leonel L. Mitchell, "Christian Initiation, Rites of Passage, and Confirmation," in Kendig Brubaker Cully, *Confirmation Re-examined* (Wilton: Morehouse-Barlow Co., 1982) 86.

42. Allen F. Bray III, "Baptism and Confirmation: A Relationship of Process," in Cully, *op. cit.* 39.

43. That baptism/confirmation were always to have been understood in this way can be perceived in the early baptismal sermons delivered to new initiants. Hippolytus in the third century preached:

And when these things have been accomplished, let each one be zealous to perform good works and to please God, living righteously, devoting himself to the Church, performing the things which he has learnt, advancing in the service of God. [Quoted in Dujarier, *The History of the Catechumenate, op. cit.* 54.]

John Chrysostom issued these words:

Imitate [Christ], I implore you, and you will be called neophytes not only for two, three, ten, or twenty days, but you will still merit this name after ten, twenty, or thirty years, and in fact for all your lives. [*Ibid.* 106.]

Chrysostom in fact compared the catechetical process itself to the environment of a wrestling school. Nothing endangers the person in the school itself—the challenge only comes afterward, when all that is learned in the school will have to be put into practice:

Let us learn, during this time of training [he therefore says], the grips [our opponent, the Evil One] uses, the source of his wickedness, and how he can easily hurt us. Then, when the contest comes, we will not be caught unaware nor be frightened, as we would be if we were to see new wrestling tricks; because we have practiced among ourselves and have learned all his artifices, we will confidently join grips with him in combat. [Quoted by Mitchell in Westerhoff & Edwards, *op. cit.* 68.]

44. Barth acknowledges that there are theological problems which accompany confirmation—e.g. does not baptism in and of itself make one a full member of the body of Christ, without needing to wait for a rite a decade or more afterward to make it so? However, he points out that the problems all arise from the practice of infant baptism itself, about which he expressed in no uncertain terms his own desire to see abolished. He asserted that there may be a "crisis in confirmation"; nonetheless, he said, "this is simply a reflection and symptom of the crisis in baptism." [Barth, *op. cit.* 189.]

45. Bray, in Cully, *op. cit.* 40.

46. Quoted in Constance J. Tarasar, "The Orthodox Experience," in Westerhoff & Edwards, *op. cit.* 255.

47. Quoted in Dujarier, *The Rites of Christian Initiation, op. cit.* 170.

48. Westerhoff & Edwards, *op. cit.* 6.

49. Aidan Kavanagh, *The Shape of Baptism: The Rite of Christian Initiation* (New York: Pueblo Publishing Company, 1978) 128.

50. Dujarier, *History of the Catechumenate, op. cit.*

51. Raymond B. Kemp, "The Rite of Christian Initiation of Adults at Ten Years," *Worship* (July 1982) 312.

52. *Book of Worship, United Church of Christ* (New York: UCC Office for Church Life & Leadership, 1986) 153.

53. Dujarier, *The Rites of Christian Initiation, op. cit.* 67.

54. William Burger and Jan Van Der Laus, "Stages of Human and Religious Growth," in Luis Malanado and David Power, *Structures of Initiation in Crisis* (New York: The Seabury Press, 1979) 43.

55. Tarasar, in Westerhoff & Edwards, *op. cit.* 256.

56. James W. Fowler, "The RCIA and Christian Religious Education," *Worship* (July 1982) 337.

57. *The Apostolic Tradition*, quoted in Dujarier, *History of the Catechumenate,* 52.

58. Leonel L. Mitchell, "The Development of Catechesis in the Third and Fourth Centuries: From Hippolytus to Augustine," in Westerhoff & Edwards, *op. cit.* 51–52.

59. Haugaard, in Westerhoff & Edwards, *op. cit.* 167.

60. Fowler, *op. cit.* 342.

61. Kemp, *op. cit.* 311.

62. Urban T. Holmes III, *Confirmation: The Celebration of Maturity in Christ* (New York: The Seabury Press, 1975) 22.

63. Dujarier, *History of the Catechumenate, op. cit.* 109.

Chapter 9

CONFIRMATION: AN EPISCOPAL CHURCH PERSPECTIVE

John H. Westerhoff III

This essay will explore theological, pastoral, cultural and catechetical insights related to confirmation and adolescence, a concern that cannot be addressed in isolation from other issues such as Christian initiation and cultural rites of passage, issues about which there is neither a single doctrinal position nor common liturgical practice in the Episcopal Church. Indeed, throughout history, Anglicanism has lacked clarity about the meaning, purpose and function of confirmation. However, while sharply different theological and pastoral points of view have been expressed and divided scholars, most have been disregarded generally by popular piety and practice.

As is commonly known confirmation as a separate sacramental rite in Christian initiation did not exist before the third century; it did not become a regular practice until after the fifth century, or a sacrament until the twelfth. Like the Roman Catholic Church, the Episcopal Church has retained the practice of baptizing its members in infancy and confirming them afterward. The rite of confirmation, however, has meant different things in different periods of history, and among the various parties (Evangelical, Anglo-Catholic, Liberal and Broad Church) which comprise the Episcopal Church. In our own day, it is at best a sacrament in search of a theology. While most every layperson, bishop, priest, and deacon has an opinion, the mind of the church is in transition. Convictions vary greatly, official statements are less than clear, and practice is vastly diverse. What follows is an attempt to name the boundaries within which the Episcopal Church now engages in confirmation.

152

The Catechism, "An Outline of the Faith" in the *Book of Common Prayer* (1979), provides an outline for instruction, a point of departure for teaching. It also provides a brief summary of the church's teaching for the inquirer. In the section on the sacraments we read that "the two great sacraments given by Christ to his Church" are baptism, "by which God adopts us as his children and makes us members of Christ's Body, the Church and inheritors of the Kingdom of God," and the holy eucharist, "commanded by Christ for the continual remembrance of his life, death, and resurrection, until his coming again" (p. 858). Then listed among the five *minor sacraments,* which "evolved in the church under the guidance of the Holy Spirit," is confirmation about which the catechism says, "[persons] express a mature commitment to Christ, and receive strength from the Holy Spirit through prayer and the laying on of hands by a bishop" (p. 860).

The *Book of Common Prayer* (1979) establishes that baptism constitutes full initiation into the church and that the bond established in baptism is indissoluble and unrepeatable. It is to be administered as a public rite in the context of the eucharist and as far as possible reserved for the Easter vigil, signifying the Pauline emphasis on baptism as death and resurrection; the day of Pentecost signifying the Lukan emphasis on baptism as receiving the Holy Spirit; the baptism of our Lord signifying the Johannine emphasis on baptism as new birth or regeneration; All Saints Day signifying baptism as reception into the community of saints; and the visitation of the bishop signifying reception into the Holy Catholic Church.

Having said that, there are two positions on Christian initiation represented in The *Book of Common Prayer* (1979). Each is based upon a different interpretation of our rites of initiation and the history that led up to their adoption.

As early as 1968 the Theological Committee of the House of Bishops, the Standing Liturgical Commission, and the Prayer Book Revision Committee agreed that baptism is the sole rite of Christian initiation, a rite which includes the laying on of hands, consignation (with or without chrism), prayer for the gift of the Holy Spirit, reception by the Christian community, a joining of the eucharistic fellowship, and commissioning for Christian ministry. When the bishop is present, the bishop is to preside; in other cases the presbyter is to preside as the bishop's representative.

It was assumed that a voluntary act, a personal acceptance of the promises and affirmations made by parents and the community for an infant, is spiritually desirable for these persons as they enter adulthood. It was also assumed that these are appropriately made in the presence of a bishop as a representative of the diocese and the Holy Catholic Church, and that on such occasions the bishop will transmit his blessings by the laying on of hands and a prayer for strengthening graces. However, in no way was this to be understood as completing holy baptism (the only pre-condition to participate in holy communion) or as conveying a special status as church members.

The committee's intention, therefore, was to restore baptism to its ancient integrity and to thereby eliminate confirmation as a separate rite, corresponding to the Eastern Orthodox model. Further, while continuing to affirm the validity and affirmation of infant baptism, it was established that the normative nature of the Christian initiation was adult or believers' baptism. Appropriate rites and catechetical processes similar to the Roman Catholic RCIA model were provided. While in principle the theology behind these proposals was affirmed, the church meeting in council could not agree on their liturgical and sacramental implications. As a consequence, the rites of initiation in the *Book of Common Prayer* (1979) and the *Book of Occasional Services,* in which the RCIA is found, provide two possible interpretations which bishops are free to adopt and practice in their diocese. The result is the establishment of two different understandings of confirmation, leaving history to judge and establish which will become the mind and the will of the church (a typical Anglican way to resolve conflict).

The first of these understandings is *confirmation outside the baptismal rite.* Confirmation outside the baptismal rite is basically a continuation of traditional practice. This understanding asserts that the minister must be a bishop and include the laying of hands with the formula: "Defend O Lord your servant *N* with your heavenly grace that *he* may continue yours forever and daily increase in your Holy Spirit more and more until *he* comes to your everlasting kingdom" (p. 309). However, while maintaining confirmation as a separate rite, it is no longer to be a prerequisite for communion. It is anticipated that this rite will be celebrated in early adolescence and be understood as the completion of baptism with an emphasis on the Holy Spirit. It is also to be used for those baptized in other denominations who have not received the Episcopal laying on of hands, and for those baptized in an Episcopal church as adults by a presbyter.

The second is *confirmation within the baptismal rite* which is a break with traditional practice, but consistent with the original will of the framers of reform. This understanding asserts that baptism is a full and complete rite of initiation and that a presbyter may be the designated minister. It is still anticipated, however, that at some later age, not earlier than late adolescence, a person is to be presented to the bishop for the laying on of hands and prayer. While still called "confirmation," the formula is changed to "Strengthen O Lord your servant *N* with your Holy Spirit and empower *him* to your services and sustain *him* all the days of *his* life" (p. 308). Another formula is provided also which may be used with adolescents baptized as infants, as well as adults baptized in the Episcopal Church and those baptized in other denominations who have not received the Episcopal laying on of hands, namely, "*N* may the Holy Spirit who has begun a good work in you direct and uphold you in the service of Christ and his kingdom" (p. 310). The emphasis in this later case is on reaffirmation of the baptismal covenant made by others and now made by an adolescent, for an adult baptized by a presbyter, and for any baptized adult who wishes to reaffirm that covenant. With this understanding, those entering the Episcopal Church who have been baptized and received the Episcopal laying on of hands in other communions enter with the formula: "*N* we recognize you as a member of the one Holy Catholic and Episcopalian church and we receive you into the fellowship of this communion, called the Father, God the Son, God the Holy Spirit bless, preserve and keep you. Amen" (p. 310).

In either case, two significant assumptions underlie the new rites of initiation. First, the establishment of adult or believers' baptism as the norm or standard by which baptism of infants is judged, and, second, the expectation that no matter when a person is baptized he or she will at a number of specific times, publicly and personally, renew his or her baptism covenant, just as the community in general will renew that covenant at the five specific occasions each year when baptisms are to be celebrated or on those same occasions even if there is no one to baptize. Confirmation, in this case, is best understood as simply the first time, at whatever age, but more than likely in the late twenties or early thirties, that a person makes the first renewal of his or her baptismal covenant.

The desire to keep adult and infant baptism with numerous renewals by both persons baptized as infants and adults is based on the following theological assumptions. In adult baptism we are baptized *on* faith; as such we are reminded that baptism is a sacrament and not magic, making real for us what is already true, that baptism calls for a personal moral response, and that baptism is a mature action not to be engaged in lightly or unadvisedly. In infant baptism we are baptized *into* faith; as such we are reminded that the church's faith comes before our own, that God's grace comes before our response, and that life is a pilgrimage of living into our baptism, of becoming who we already are.

The *Book of Common Prayer* (1979) strives to maintain the tension between these two understandings and their complex relationship through two rubrics.

The first is that all baptized persons are to renew the baptismal covenant five times each year, at the Easter vigil, the day of Pentecost, All Saints Day, the baptism of our Lord, and the visitation of the bishop, even if there is no one to be baptized (p. 312).

The second is that "in the course of their Christian development, those baptized at an early age are expected, when they are ready and have been duly prepared, to make a mature public affirmation of the faith, and commitment to the responsibilities of their baptism and to receive the laying on of hands by the bishop" (p. 412). It is assumed that this action will be repeated throughout one's life and with significant catechetical preparation.

To return to the rubric just mentioned, it appears, at least to me, that "when ready" implies physical, psycho-social and mental development rather than chronological age; that "duly prepared" implies a serious educational experience commensurate to the action being taken; that a "mature" act implies that a person has attained at least an advanced state of growth and development; that a "public affirmation of faith" implies the ability to intellectually declare and defend the fundamental convictions underlying the Christian faith and life; and that a "commitment to the responsibilities of baptism" implies the ability to make a rational, binding promise to act as a believer in Jesus Christ and a member of his church.

Therefore, on the basis of this *Book of Common Prayer* (1979) understanding of confirmation as baptismal renewal, adolescence is an inappropriate age for this sacrament to be celebrated because it asks more than is possible for persons between the ages of twelve and twenty-one; it tends to deter or put closure on an essential lifelong growth process which occurs during this period; it has the possibility of manipulating persons into unfaithful, immoral actions; it meets at best legitimate human needs in an improper theological-moral-sacramental manner; and last it suggests an implicit teaching about the sacraments that is theologically questionable.

First, adolescence (ages twelve to twenty-one) is inappropriate for the sacrament of confirmation because it asks more than persons between these ages can deliver. Until the modern period the world was divided neatly between childhood and adulthood. In our own century it was discovered that there was a ten year period of social transition as well as psychological and mental development during the years between childhood and adulthood, a somewhat lengthy period necessary for persons to acquire a new set of capacities for self-awareness, interpersonal relations and cognitive processes, along with a necessary social delay in assuming adult responsibility for their lives. As such, this period which was named adolescence requires that while we lay solid foundations for later decision making, we encourage a moratorium on as many serious decisions as possible. Insofar as confirmation calls for a mature decision and response of affirmation and commitment, adolescence becomes an important period for the development of these capacities rather than the making of a response which will be better made sometime during early adulthood (in the late twenties to early thirties) when persons can at least *begin* to assume mature responsibility for their faith and life. To expect an adolescent to make these responses without the necessary growth and learning to do so is to expect too much.

Second, adolescence is an inappropriate age for confirmation because when celebrated at this age it tends to deter or put closures on an essential growth process. Christian life is comprised of numerous moments of transition and growth. Christians need to be confirmed in that lifelong growth and aided during transitions to identify more deeply with the church and participate more fully in its mission and ministry. Adolescence is an important and necessary transitional period in human growth in our society, and adolescents need to be confirmed in that growth by the church. Nevertheless, confirmation practiced during the teen years tends to work against such needs by suggesting a finalization or graduation exercise. As Jesus' parable of the two sons (Mt 21:28–32) makes clear, God wants our capacity to say "no" as a pre-condition of our saying "yes." To ask for a "yes" before one has had the opportunity to say "no" stifles the process. Many insist that they do offer adolescents a choice, but while some youth may be able to act on conscience, parental, parish and even peer expectations make it extremely difficult if not impossible. A response of faith made during these years is more than likely to stifle growth in faith rather than encourage it. Worst, an unhealthy guilt about saying "yes" when not convinced or "no" in the face of immaturity can result in an inability to grow in faith.

Third, adolescence is an inappropriate age for confirmation because during these years it has the potential of manipulating persons into unfaithful, immoral acts. A moral act is an act of personal loyalty, conviction and commitment made freely on the basis of knowledge and awareness following serious reflection. During adolescence persons only are in the process of developing the capacities and skills necessary for decision making. They only are beginning to acquire the knowledge and experience necessary for making a reasonable decision. Further, they are unduly influenced by significant others, adult authority figures, and peers. Adolescence is a time for encountering new experiences and perspectives and for trying on new beliefs, attitudes and behaviors. It is a time for learning what it means to make decisions, to act upon them, and to take responsibility for their consequences. It is a time for persons to begin to assume responsibility for their own faith and life, but not for reaching decisions or stating convictions and commitments on faith and life. Childhood is a time for exploring convictions through intellectual conversions and nurture in theological reflection. Adulthood, therefore, is a more appropriate time for such actions.

Fourth, adolescence is an inappropriate age for confirmation because it at best addresses legitimate needs in an improper manner. Many bishops desire significant contact with adolescents in their parishes so as to minister to them and assist them in establishing an Episcopal identity. Many priests desire significant contact with adolescents so as to ensure that they will have a strong foundation for faith and life. Many parents and other adults desire adolescents to be confirmed so that they may fulfill their baptismal promise to bring their children up in the Christian faith and life. Others are concerned that the church does everything in its power to nurture and protect youth in the faith and life of the church during these difficult transitional years. These are all legitimate concerns. However, for any action to be justified both ends and means need to be considered. The price to be paid for attempting to meet these needs through the rite of confirmation is extremely high. More important, there are other, better ways to meet these needs which we will discuss later.

And fifth, adolescence is an inappropriate age for confirmation because it carries with it an implicit teaching about the sacraments which is theologically questionable. Relating baptism and confirmation to the life cycle events of birth and maturation produces numerous difficulties in that one's personal public confession of Christian faith at confirmation implies that it is more important than baptism. The presence and action of the bishop at confirmation with all the power and authority of that office diminishes the significance of baptism. This turns baptism into little more than a preliminary rite of exorcism from sin and inflates confirmation into a de facto surrogate baptism administered in the midst of the adolescent psycho-social identity crisis.

More serious, confirmation in adolescence gives the impression that baptism is an incomplete sacrament which requires completion. Baptism, however, is a complete act of initiation into the Christian community. Every baptized person is a member of the church and welcome to participate at its sacred meal, the eucharist. Baptism needs nothing to complete it or perfect it. It is the church's rite of full initiation into the body of Christ. Christian faith and life established at baptism does require a response, or, better, numerous responses, general or particular, throughout one's life, but the responses are always secondary to the act of baptism. No one response (e.g. confirmation) is complete or fully satisfactory. We are always living into the truth of our baptism, we are always responding to God's grace in our lives, we are always renewing and reaffirming our vows and covenant, we are always becoming who and whose we are already.

It is essential for us to remember that adolescence is a modern sociological and psychological phenomenon found only in complex industrial societies. In 1904 G. Stanley Hall wrote a book entitled *Adolescence* to describe a new psychological phenomenon. However, in most societies persons move from childhood to adulthood in a single move. Rites of passage or transition were established to aid that change in role and status. But in our society where adolescence lasts for more than a decade there is no single public rite that has meaning. Still the cultural need for passage from childhood and adulthood persists, and many have assumed or tried to make confirmation fill that important social role. But confirmation is not and never has been a rite of passage from one role and status to another. Confirmation is a rite of intensification, affirming role and status previously established at baptism. As such, it is conceivably a repeatable rite appropriate whenever one wishes to engage in it, aiding an individual to affirm and reestablish his or her role and status as a baptized person. Insofar as confirmation can never satisfy the needs of an adolescent, persons in our society during these years are left with a psycho-social void to be replaced by unhealthy rites of passage sometimes related to driving the car, engaging in intercourse, drinking alcoholic beverages or using drugs, and so forth.

A healthy rite of passage or transition has certain characteristics. The rite itself begins with a ritual/ceremonial separation from one's current status and role, followed by a period of transition characterized by the experience of liminality (being betwixt and between), ordeal (leading to an experience of "communitas"), and formation (preparation for one's new role and status). The rite ends with a second ritual/ceremonial which reincorporates the person into the community in his or her new status and role.

The marriage rite provides a simple illustration, but in conflict with contemporary practice. The first ritual/ceremonial is the engagement. It is followed by a period in which the two persons act as neither single nor married. It proceeds through a period of ordeal in which the couple is bound together and prepared for their new status as married persons and their new roles as husband and wife. The rite ends with a wedding ritual/ceremonial and honeymoon from which they return as a married couple. Of course, in our day this rite is often distorted insofar as persons live together before they are engaged, the engagement is too short for appropriate preparation, and there is no ordeal insofar as they tend to behave as if they are already married, but that is another issue for another time.

In most simple societies there is a rite of passage for boys and girls which is intended to aid their movement from childhood to adulthood, a process which involves a liminal ordeal of separation from the community and a process of enculturation or formation so that they may be fashioned into persons able to function as adults in the community. A society which lacks such rites becomes dysfunctional, and persons who do not have the experiences of such rites tend to manifest unhealthy behavior.

Our society needs badly to create a true rite of passage *for* adolescence, which is very different from a rite of passage *from* childhood to adulthood. The church in its history has developed rites to meet life cycle needs. Today we need to create a new one for adolescence and separate it from confirmation.

What follows is an outline for a suggestion of such a rite and its necessary catechetical component.

Adolescents in our culture and society require a rite of responsibility. Somewhere around seventh or eighth grade or twelve years of age the church needs to celebrate a ritual/ceremonial in which boys and girls are separated from childhood and officially inducted into the beginning of adolescence. It might best take place on their birthday and would be seen as an individual rite similar to the bar or batmitzvah in the Jewish tradition. Parents would present their child to the community and pray a public prayer thanking God for taking away the full burden and responsibility of their child's faith and conduct, as well as asking for the graces needed to be present to and support their child as he or she moves through adolescence into adulthood. The child would make a statement before the community accepting the ordeal of learning to be responsible for her or his own faith and life. The community would give each child a gift, such as a Bible, to guide each one on the way. A sponsor, an adult other than the parents, chosen by the community and the child, would be presented and commissioned to be responsible for accompanying the child on his or her pilgrimage.

Somewhere around twelfth grade or eighteen years of age the church would celebrate a second ritual/ceremonial in which the adolescent would be separated from adolescence and inducted into the beginnings of adulthood. Again it would take place on his or her birthday and would be an event in which the sponsor presents the young man or woman to the community, summarizing his or her preparation, accomplishments and promise. Such youths should make a statement on their readiness to assume responsibility for their faith and life and promise at an appropriate time in the future to renew their baptismal vows and covenant following significant preparation. During the service they would assume an adult role such as reading a lesson in the liturgy and perhaps would choose a saint they would like to emulate and be given a symbol of their life with a charge to assume responsibility for their faith and life and prayers for the graces needed to do. An appropriate party would follow.

During this eight year period a program, part personal and part social, would be developed to aid adolescents to be able to assume responsibility for their own faith and life. It would be radically different from any learning experiences or learning contexts found in childhood or adulthood. It would include *forma-*

tion through the practice and experience of responsible Christian faith and life, *education* through the critical reflection on their practice and experience in the light of scripture and tradition, and *instruction* through which they would acquire the knowledge and skills necessary for responsible Christian faith and life such as being able to interpret, think theologically and make moral decisions.

If we can give birth to such a rite and its related catechetical process, I suspect we will experience few dropouts during adolescence. Further, the period of young adulthood would present us with persons ready and able to begin their preparation for the first renewal of their baptism, or "confirmation." Parenthetically, the catechetical process for baptismal renewal already exists in the Episcopal Church in *Living Into Our Baptism* developed by Caroline Hughes, canon for education in the diocese of Atlanta, and myself.

To summarize, the Episcopal Church is convinced it needs to remove confirmation from adolescence and provide an alternative rite for adolescence. Only if we are able to do so will confirmation maintain its integrity, however understood.

Of course, the fundamental issue remains: confirmation needs to be returned to the rite of baptism and numerous occasions related to the life cycle and human life crises seen as opportunities for baptismal renewal, preceded by significant catechetical preparation. Until this occurs, I and others in the Episcopal Church suspect that the rite of adolescent confirmation will continue to plague us, causing theologians to strive to find a defense, and catechists a means to prepare persons for participation.

RESOURCES

Other sources of insight into issue of Christian initiation and confirmation in the Episcopal Churches are A. Theodore Eastman, *The Baptizing Community;* Kendig B. Cully (ed.), *Confirmation Re-Examined;* Urban T. Holmes, *Confirmation;* Marion Hatchett, *Commentary on the American Prayer Book;* Charles Price and Louis Weil, *Liturgy for Living;* and Daniel B. Stevick, *Baptismal Moments; Baptismal Meanings.*

Further, for five years, from 1977 to 1981, I have explored various issues related to adolescence and confirmation. Resultant articles and book chapters contain the roots of my present argument: see "Betwixt and Between," *Liturgy,* Winter 1977; "Joining the Church or Witnessing to Faith," *Character Potential,* Spring-Summer 1978; "Identity and Pilgrimage of Faith," in *Learning Through Liturgy* (New York: Seabury, 1979); "Personal Growth in Identity," *Learning Through the Life Cycle,* Westerhoff and Willimon (New York: Seabury, 1980); "Framing an Alternative Future for Confirmation," *A Faithful Church,* Westerhoff and Edwards (New York: Moorehouse-Barlow, 1981); "Aspects of Adolescent Confirmation," in *Confirmation Re-Examined,* Kendig Cully (ed.) (New York: Moorehouse-Barlow, 1982).

Chapter 10

RETHINKING CONFIRMATION: POSSIBLE WAYS FORWARD

Craig Cox

It is obvious that an impasse exists over confirmation.

Perhaps the biggest problem in the theological debate is the seemingly irreconcilable conflict between two positions on the meaning of confirmation. One position, which is found in most of the academic writing on the subject, sees confirmation as part of an initiation ritual that must—to be true to its theological and historical foundations—follow baptism and precede eucharist. . . . The other position, which informs most of the sacramental practice in the American church, sees confirmation as a ceremony in which the initiation of one who was baptized in infancy is affirmed, ratified, "confirmed" by one mature enough to make an informed commitment.[1]

A choice one way or the other will leave the proponents of the opposite point of view dissatisfied. Given the terms under which the issue has been discussed, there seems no happy solution. But this must prod us to question those terms.

This leads to our first question. Doesn't this impasse reveal the need to adopt a much more radical approach to cut through the problems? Do we not need to reexamine some presuppositions to see if, just possibly, there is a deeper ground on which a convergence of views is possible? Given the fruitlessness of the present debate, it seems clear that a new start is needed. We are bogged down, and doomed to remain so, unless we step back to see if there might be some way in which the values and goals of opposing views can not only be preserved, but actually brought into a creative synthesis.

This prepares for our second question. Should not the traditional link of the sacraments of initiation be restored and fostered by a unified celebration of baptism and confirmation? This is the position of many in the church today:

> . . . the liturgists consider that ever since Confirmation was split off from Baptism and later from First Holy Communion, it has been a poor orphan in the Church, deprived of its status and meaning.[2]

A solution is offered by John Nuttall to save this "poor orphan":

> A view gaining ground among liturgists, and my own view, is that, in addition to the Adult Rite, we should also opt for infant baptism with confirmation and eucharist at the same time.[3]

Given what we have learned from our historical survey about the almost accidental separation of the rites of initiation, this view seems reasonable. While some, such as William Marrevee,[4] argue quite cogently that the link between the sacraments does not depend on their chronological unity, I believe we can and should recognize that, in fact, the interrelation of baptism and confirmation is not popularly appreciated. Thus, the concerns of liturgists and others are genuine; a chronological reunion of the three sacraments has a great value. But while affirming this truth, I hasten to emphasize that it is not the whole truth; there is a wider picture.

In assessing the historical processes that have led to a separate rite of confirmation, some see a tragedy.

> When I refer to the breakdown or disintegration of initiation, I have in mind the dismemberment of the ritual elements . . . into distinct sacramental moments separated by intervals of time.[5]

But this opinion is challenged by a third question: Isn't it possible, even likely, that the Spirit has been working in the gradual separation of confirmation from baptism? Was this not a legitimate development rather than a "disintegration" or "dismemberment"? Jerome Bertram reflects along these same lines:

> . . . we can see how it was appropriate to give it [Confirmation] immediately after Baptism for an adult convert, but that it may well have been a mistake to attach it so closely to Baptism that, after infant baptism became normal, Confirmation followed suit. In which case the Holy Spirit, working through the whole People of God, has been working to return it to a place on the threshold of adulthood.[6]

Catholics believe in the ongoing guidance of the Spirit. Our new historical understanding helps us appreciate that Jesus and the early church did not give us a blueprint, but a vision. Before rejecting the practice that has developed over the centuries, we need to gauge not how it conforms to one stage in history, but how it conforms to and serves that vision inspired by the Spirit. In speaking precisely of this, Kieran Sawyer observes:

> . . . an increasing number of American bishops are delaying the age for confirmation to late adolescence or early adulthood. One of those bishops is Rembert Weakland, OSB, Archbishop of Milwaukee. . . . Weakland believes that the practice of delaying confirmation represents an evolution in the understanding of initiation that has been guided by the Spirit in response to a very real pastoral need . . . he states, "I am hesitant to cast aside all theological development concerning Confirmation and the Initiation Rites that took place from the catechumenate period to the present day as being somehow unimportant and insignificant and not inspired by a logical principle."[7]

As the cliché reminds us, God can "write straight with crooked lines." While the present practice of confirmation may have seemed to develop accidentally, many believe that a deeper wisdom was at work.

> The reasons for delaying confirmation now, however, are not the same reasons as those which led to the original separation. They are based on sound theological grounds; in fact, they are

the very principles most stressed by the Constitution on the Liturgy—the fully conscious and active participation of the faithful in the liturgy.[8]

Buckley goes on to conclude:

> . . . at what age should confirmation be given to those who are baptized in infancy? It should be given when they have sufficient psychological and spiritual maturity. For most Catholics, this will occur around the time they leave school and enter the world of business and labor.[9]

Might not God be leading the church to a fuller view of human initiation and a richer sacramental celebration of the reality of initiation precisely through the felt needs for rites of passage and adult commitment? Again, many answer "yes!" But this too is not the whole truth; it is only part of the complete answer to our dilemma.

A fourth series of questions remains. With our new appreciation for the human dimension of the sacraments, we must ask: Can we not learn some important truths from the persons who celebrate initiation that will help us see the nature and role of confirmation? Does not an appreciation of psychological studies about "stages of growth" in human life give us some insight? After all, to paraphrase the gospel, the sacraments are made for people, not people for the sacraments.[10]

> Instead of deciding first what is theologically right on Confirmation and applying it to present-day candidates, it might be more sound theologically and more in the spirit of the Incarnation if we were to start with the psychological and emotional needs and development of the young person, as well as relevant sociological factors, now that we have an increasing insight into these areas available to us, and proceed from that point to discover what is theologically right about Confirmation . . . . Our theological task, then, is not to discover a theology and apply it, but to discover the needs of the growing adolescent and meet them. In meeting these needs we

will discover what is theologically right for our situation and age.[11]

The studies of developmental psychologists and many of the popularized accounts based on these studies make us more aware that there are stages or "passages" throughout life. The transitions between each stage present challenges or "tasks" that must be addressed if human growth is to continue.

> When the old is broken and the new has not yet come, we must venture out into the unknown. These are the passages of our lives. All passages are times of crisis. All times of crisis are marked by unusual opportunities and unusual dangers. . . . In order to maximize the promise of the opportunities and minimize the threat of the dangers, humans throughout the ages have created *rites* to accompany life's major passages.[12]

Our human identity is shaped by these times of crisis, and thus, if grace builds on nature, our identity as Christians is shaped by them as well. Tremendous implications follow if we take these insights seriously. Just as human growth is ongoing (Elisabeth Kübler-Ross aptly entitled one book, *Death: The Final Stage of Growth*), so is Christian initiation. It too is not completed until, through death, we come to resurrected life. How does the church respond to this? What "rites" allow us to maximize the opportunities here? Is not our older view of initiation—at least the way we celebrated it sacramentally—inadequate in the face of this reality? Is not "confirming the faith" an ongoing need for humans, a need that takes different shapes and provides different challenges at different stages on our life journeys? Of course, the answer is "yes," a yes that challenges our sacramental system of initiation.

A Not So Modest Proposal

Strong arguments buttress an affirmative response to the questions just discussed. But is it possible to affirm them all? Are they not, at least to a substantial degree, mutually exclusive? As with all paradoxes, at first it does seem impossible to reconcile these affirmations. But I am convinced there is a solution that respects those positions, fosters the values underlying them, and cuts through the impasse over confirmation.

I propose that we rethink the tradition of having only one celebration of confirmation in life. Would it not be more appropriate to celebrate the one ongoing sacramental reality of "confirming faith" in several stages at critical junctures in life, with a catechesis and ritual appropriate to the needs of people in those periods? Such a proposal is radical but, as I will argue below, it does preserve the key values of the major schools of thought on confirmation. What is more, it offers the possibility of a richer sacramental experience in adult years, as well as providing a sturdy framework upon which to build a comprehensive process of adult religious education. If Gunter Biemer is correct about the 'impossibility of establishing any one specific age at which the psychological and sociological prerequisites for confirmation are met,[13] then doesn't this suggest God may be leading us to celebrate confirmation in stages at different ages?

Recently, others have begun to think along similar lines. The Episcopal Church's new *Book of Common Prayer* provides for a rite of reaffirmation which tries to address the same concerns.[14] William Horton also speaks of the ongoing need for confirming faith.

> Where confirmation is concerned, the Christian may receive confirmation of God's grace at many times and in many ways during his life and, by that same grace, may confirm his faith at many times and in many ways, but at one time the special way of confirmation is to be received as a gift of God, symbolic and determinative of all the others.[15]

Horton understands both the ongoing need within people as well as God's continuing confirming action in human life, but he has not yet questioned the presupposition that there can be only one sacramental celebration of this reality. And yet, our review of sacramentology shows that sacraments are celebrations precisely of what God is doing in life. Further, we have come to appreciate the process dimension of human life and Christian initiation. If in truth God confirms us and deepens our initiation multiple times, why not celebrate this truth, thus strengthening its impact, bringing that grace to greater conscious awareness, and giving thanks to God for this gift?

Jerome Bertram comes closer to suggesting such a conclusion when he reflects:

> There is of course a possibility of combining the best of both worlds: often in an "either-or" debate the Catholic answer is "both." Is it possible to envisage more than one moment of anointing rather as is the practice of the Orthodox Church? . . . we are already familiar with the idea of renewing a sacrament . . . could not Confirmation be renewed when an adult, perhaps after lapsing, wishes to return to his faith? After all, we anticipate Confirmation in the rite of infant Baptism, at the anointing with chrism.[16]

But Bertram, too, stops short of advocating actually celebrating the sacrament of confirmation in stages, primarily because he fears violating the "sacramental character" of confirmation.

Putting aside objections and questions for a moment, let us focus on what confirmation might look like if this proposal were to win acceptance. How could it accomplish the goal of preserving the values of each school of thought? First, the present anointing with chrism at the baptism of infants would be expanded into the first stage of confirmation. (In some respects, isn't that precisely what it is, even though we have not given it the name?) This would enable the church to reunite the ancient ritual of initiation, for, as in the eastern tradition, first eucharist should be celebrated here as well. It would also offer a clearer witness to the action of the Spirit in Christian initiation by eliminating the problem of distinguishing different "ways" in which the Spirit is given that has been so troublesome. The ritual of this unified celebration would also strongly emphasize the fact that it begins a process in which other stages follow, that the gift of God bestowed in baptism and confirmed for the life-stage of infancy (or for whatever life-stage the newly baptized is experiencing) will require further growth and ongoing confirmation. A second stage might occur around the time we now celebrate first communion and penance, the age of discretion of long tradition and present canon law. A third stage could be celebrated at roughly the same time that is so common in the United States as a rite of passage for the tumultuous period of adolescence. As we have seen, many point out how deeply a person's identity is shaped in these years and how desperately faith needs to be confirmed at this age. A fourth stage could occur sometime in young adulthood, as that mature profession of faith for which many cry.[17] A fifth stage might be appropriate during the challenges of the so-called "mid-life crisis," for in this period too people face spiritual challenges and are called to a deeper incorporation into Christ. Finally, a sixth stage might be celebrated sometime in "old age." As faith is tested by the progressive weakening of the mind and body and the steady approach of death, we certainly need to be confirmed and grow more into the likeness of the Christ who "emptied himself" and was crucified as prelude to his exaltation. Not every person need celebrate every stage, and these suggestions can certainly be debated and modified. For now, the particulars are not as important as catching the vision and a sense of the marvelous possibilities inherent in a move in this direction.

It is time, however, to discuss the major obstacles facing such a proposal. Three extremely significant objections must be addressed. The first is simple and straightforward. A centuries-long tradition exists of a single celebration of confirmation; how can we even think of putting aside that tradition? Yet the tradition itself provides a response. In early centuries, the celebration of sacramental penance and reconciliation was also understood as a once in a lifetime reality. Karl Rahner describes the second century practice:

> In view of the imminent end of the world, Hermas proclaims just one further possible penance [after baptism], but he is by no means the first to open up this possibility. Hermas' once and for all penance . . . became a principle of penitential practice in the West for the whole of the patristic age. . . .[18]

Speaking of the later patristic age, Rahner continues:

> The West maintains even more radically that there is only a single possibility of church penance. . . . In practice penance is more and more postponed to the death-bed and this prac-

tice is even approved; synods warn against undertaking
church penance before a mature age, since this—because of
the once and for all nature and the lasting consequences of
church penance—would be bound to lead to insoluble con-
flicts. . . . Thus, there is often an anxious effort to achieve
reconciliation with the Church just before death.[19]

As is obvious from today's practice, this tradition of the earliest
centuries was revised in response to the needs of people and because of a realization that the practice unduly limited God's
mercy. If the church could grow to understand penance in a new
way which led to the conviction that multiple celebrations were
part of God's plan, it seems we have a precedent upon which to
base a similar change with confirmation.

But at this point, a second and more difficult objection is
posed. There is a difference between penance and confirmation,
in that the later is said to possess a special "sacramental character." This truth was defined by the Council of Florence in 1439:

> Among the sacraments, there are three, baptism, confirma-
> tion and holy orders, which print on the soul an indelible
> character, that is, a certain spiritual sign distinguishing the
> recipient from others. Hence, these are not given more than
> once to one person.[20]

The Council of Trent reiterates this, adding the following canon:

> 9. If anyone says that in these three sacraments, namely, bap-
> tism, confirmation and holy orders, a character is not im-
> printed on the soul—that is, a kind of indelible spiritual sign
> whereby these sacraments cannot be repeated: let him be
> anathema.[21]

This seems to slam the door shut on this proposal, or does it?
Note that these definitions speak of three sacraments which imprint a character and thus supposedly can be received only once.
Confirmation and baptism are joined with holy orders in this
respect. However, theology and official church teaching has not

found these conciliar definitions an impediment to a celebration of the one sacrament of holy orders in three grades or stages, at different times in the life of the same person. The Apostolic Constitution of Paul VI in the 1968 revision of the Rite of Ordination speaks of this:

> Among the rites of ordinations the first to be considered are those which constitute the hierarchy through the sacrament of Order, conferred in several grades. . . .[22]

I have been speaking of a similar appreciation of confirmation. This is one sacrament, but I believe its very nature demands that it be celebrated in stages which lead to a greater and greater fullness of initiation, just as the stages of holy orders lead to the fullness of priesthood. Thus, the sacramental character of confirmation and the definitions of Florence and Trent are not insurmountable obstacles should the church judge that the Spirit is leading us to accept this proposed new practice of confirmation.

A third objection would argue that such a proposal undermines the role of the eucharist as the celebration of ongoing initiation. A. Theodore Eastman asserts that "the Eucharist has been the regular occasion by which Christians renew their baptismal commitment to God."[23] Indeed, the eucharist is one of the three sacraments of initiation, and its role as an ongoing celebration of our incorporation into Christ is clear. This must be preserved in any reform of confirmation along the lines we have been discussing. But that is not to say that eucharist is the only such celebration needed. Eastman himself recognizes this:

> . . . it also makes sense to provide other formal occasions and mechanisms for mature Christians to renew their basic baptismal commitments, perhaps more than once during the course of a lifetime.[24]

There is a difference between normal everyday growth and those special or critical stages that occur as milestones in the midst of ordinary experience. The eucharist, under its symbolism as nourishment, and because it can be celebrated so frequently, is particularly suited to sanctify our day-in, day-out growth. But it is not as well suited to give special focus and attention to those critical milestones and life passages. A way is needed to deal with these critical junctures sacramentally, in order to address the extraordinary and unique challenges they pose. Thus, a celebration of confirmation in stages would serve to complement the eucharist in its role as an ongoing celebration of initiation, not undermine or compete with it.

It seems, then, that these objections may not pose insurmountable problems should the church choose radically to rethink confirmation. Of course, other proposals have been made to deal with these concerns. One suggestion is to delay baptism, enrolling infants as catechumens and at a later age celebrating the sacraments of initiation in a unified rite.[25] But the question arises: "At what age?" Any choice (age of discretion, adolescence, young adulthood) has its serious drawbacks. Also, a goal of the liturgical theologians proposing this is to build an appreciation of initiation as a process. Yet might not putting all the sacramental rites together tend to detract from such an appreciation in the mind of the average "person in the pew"? A second suggestion is to create new but non-sacramental rites to celebrate later life passages, somewhat along the lines of the Episcopal Church's rite of reaffirmation mentioned earlier.[26] But has that rite had much impact in Episcopal congregations? Why limit ourselves to a non-sacramental rite? If we truly believe that initiation is a lifelong process and that God is working throughout that process, then let us sacramentalize it fully. My hunch is that non-sacramental rites would not appeal to the great majority of people in our congregations; the sacrament of confirmation celebrated in stages, on the other hand, could have a much wider appeal.

I am convinced that this is the lesson the Spirit is teaching in the so-called "disintegration" of the initiation rites. The original rite has disintegrated. But in the context of the paschal mystery, isn't it likely that this "death" will lead to a much fuller "life," that the ancient and beautiful but inadequate process of initiation will finally be refashioned into a truly lifelong sacramental process?

Conclusion

I will be the first to admit that this "not so modest proposal" is a drastic one. But rethinking confirmation in this way opens some impressive vistas. I do not pretend that it is an easy or problem-free solution, but I do believe it is one that should be given serious consideration and study. In the face of the impasse over confirmation, in which the various pastoral practices and theological positions have not been able to be reconciled, such a radical solution may be exactly what is needed.

NOTES

1. Sawyer, "Toward an Integrated Theology," p. 336.
2. Michael Gwinnell, "Confirmation: Sacrament of Initiation," *The Clergy Review*, 1970, p. 126.
3. John C. Nuttall, "Confirmation: At What Age?" *The Clergy Review*, 1982, p. 280.
4. William Marrevee, S.C.J., "Confirmation: A Conflict between Theology and Pastoral Practice?" *Eglise et Theologie*, 1972, p. 234.
5. Nathan Mitchell, "Christian Initiation: Decline and Dismemberment," *Worship*, 1974, pp. 459–60.
6. Jerome Bertram, "The Age For Confirmation: A Continuing Debate," *The Clergy Review*, 1982, p. 447.
7. Sawyer, "Toward an Integrated Theology," pp. 339–40.
8. Francis J. Buckley, "What Age for Confirmation?" *Theological Studies* 27 (1966) p. 660.
9. Ibid., p. 666.
10. Bernard Cooke, in *Sacraments & Sacramentality* entitles the first chapter, "Sacraments Are For Humans," and argues in that chapter for remembering that the sacraments are for people.
11. Michael Perry, ed., *Crisis for Confirmation* (London: SCM Press, 1967), pp. 187–88.
12. William O. Roberts, Jr., "Christianity's Lost Rite: Initiation to Adulthood," *The Christian Ministry*, 1983, p. 24.
13. Gunter Biemer, "Controversy on the Age of Confirmation as a Typical Example of Conflict between the Criteria of Theology and the Demands of Pastoral Practice," in *Liturgy and Human Passage*, eds.

David Power and Luis Maldonado (New York: The Seabury Press, 1979), p. 116.

14. *The Book of Common Prayer* (New York, 1979), pp. 413–19.

15. William D. Horton, "The Pastor's Problems: XIX. Confirmation," *The Expository Times,* 1983, p. 357.

16. Bertram, "The Age for Confirmation," p. 445.

17. Dan Grippo, "Confirmation: No One Under 18 Need Apply," *U.S. Catholic,* 1982, pp. 31–32. For another person holding this view, refer again to Buckley, "What Age?"

18. Karl Rahner, "The History of Penance," *Theological Investigations,* vol. 15, *Penance in the Early Church* (New York: The Crossroad Publishing Company, 1982), pp. 8–9.

19. Ibid., p. 12. It is interesting to note that in discussing the historical development of penance (pp. 10–11), Rahner explains that in the east stages of penance are elaborated, and that sometimes there is even an anointing "which later evokes the idea of a repetition of confirmation."

20. From the decree *Exultate Deo* of the Council of Florence as found in Clarkson, *The Church Teaches,* section 663.

21. From the "Canons on the Sacraments in General" of the Council of Trent as found in Clarkson, *The Church Teaches,* section 673.

22. *The Rite of Ordination* (Collegeville: The Liturgical Press, 1969), p. 5.

23. A. Theodore Eastman, *The Baptizing Community: Christian Initiation and the Local Congregation* (New York: The Seabury Press, 1982), p. 27.

24. Ibid., pp. 27–28.

25. Murphy Center for Liturgical Research, *Made, Not Born: New Perspectives on Christian Initiation and the Catechumenate* (Notre Dame: Notre Dame University Press, 1976). Several of the contributors to this collection recommend study of this option. See especially the comments by Ralph A. Kiefer, "Christian Initiation: The State of the Question," pp. 140–141 and Robert W. Hovda, "Hope for the Future: A Summary," pp. 158–59 and pp. 165–66.

26. Kiefer, "Christian Initiation," in Murphy Center for Liturgical Research, *Made, Not Born,* p. 141.

AN AFTERWORD

Bernard Cooke

What does one say in an "afterword" to a collection of essays that reflect so much of my own thinking about the sacrament of confirmation. It is much like reaching the end of the eucharistic prayer: the only suitable thing to say is "Amen." However, like the eucharistic "Amen" this volume is open-ended and eschatological; it points to life yet unlived, to commitments to be honored, to history to be created in freedom, to the yet fuller realization of the kingdom of God. The essays of this volume are not a final word, as their authors themselves state; rather, they describe and analyze the new dawn in Christian initiation ritual that has occurred in the past few decades and they point to what we hope will occur in the full light of day. Which means that there is room to explore further the paths opened up by the authors of this book, suggesting what I believe could be done to accomplish their hopes and ambitions and justify their judgments and insights.

It is clear from these essays that in theological discussion about Christian initiation the notion of *process* is "in." All of the essays in one way or another insist that confirmation must not be seen as an isolated ritual, one sacred moment of sanctification and vocation. Theresa Viramontes-Gutierrez goes further by indicating the coincidence of "process" with the biblical theme of "journey" as exemplified in the Emmaus narrative. Christian initiation is a years-long process of people coming to mature faith and committed discipleship. Confirmation is meant to fit somehow into this process of an individual becoming a Christian—or perhaps it would be more faithful to several of the essays to say that the process is one of individuals and communities becoming Christian.

Obviously this stress on process has been strongly influenced by the official restoration of the catechumenate in the RCIA. More broadly, awareness of things and people existing and acting developmentally has marked almost every aspect of human understanding in the past century; it is part of our worldview to think of the world and human society as *becoming,* i.e. in process. Still, when we speak of process as it touches on confirmation and more broadly as it describes the entirety of Christian initiation we are dealing with a unique kind of becoming. As a result, there are limits to which the general laws of psychological or societal development can be applied to Christian initiation and used as guides for understanding or creating the liturgy of confirmation.

Several of the authors already highlight this point, so there is no purpose in pursuing it. Rather, what I would like to explore further is the *nature* of the process in question. Granted that there must be a process of growth toward mature Christian faith, what kind of a process is this?

Much of the answer to this question has been provided by Kieran Sawyer as she lays the principles that should guide the preparation of adolescents for confirmation, by several authors' emphasis on development of affectivity along with knowledge, by Lynn Neu's description of the way in which the Milwaukee program leads young persons to discover themselves and one another as Christians. What I feel needs more emphasis—and I am certain that several of the authors, if given more space, would have dealt with it—is the confirmand's development of *personal friendship with the risen Christ.* All the other elements of growth must be there: clearer and more extensive understanding of the various elements of Christian belief, growing appreciation for and identity with the Christian community to which one belongs, acceptance of responsibility for the well-being of others as well as oneself, commitment to discipleship. But all these pertain to faith in proportion as they flow from a genuine friendship with Christ now.

In describing the Milwaukee preparation for the confirmation ritual, Lynn Neu underlines the effect of the retreat in which the young people engaged. My guess is that the special power of this retreat comes precisely because in it the confirmands have the experience—perhaps for the first time—of dealing with Jesus personally in their prayer. It has been my own experience that even in the somewhat artificial academic situation of the classroom there is a resonance with the mention of Christ that one does not feel when discussing any other topic. And I believe that almost all of us who deal with young people have frequently heard remarks such as "I don't buy much of what goes on in the church, but Jesus himself—that's a different matter."

What does this say about the kind of preparation that should lead up to a confirmation ritual, or for that matter about the appropriate age of confirmation? What it says is that one discovers friends and grows in their friendship throughout one's life, that different stages of friendships are possible at different ages, that the development at each age is desirable or even necessary for the relationship to endure, and that deepening friendship comes by constant loving association with the friend and not through abstract talk about the friend. Or to put it quite simply in the case of young Christians: while study and exhortation and good example have their role, the "payoff" comes in personal prayer—which, incidentally, can be either individual or shared prayer.

Again, we have to keep in mind that it is less important to talk about the church, even as a familiar and supporting community of shared goals, than to find means of making the risen Christ a reality in their experience. However, there is not really a conflict or for that matter a separation of these two goals, because the genuinely caring Christian community is itself a sacrament of the loving and saving presence of the Lord. It is in the context of a true Christian community and only there that any of us can come to personal acquaintance with Christ in faith.

Unless I am mistaken, this is what Richard Reichert is after when in his essay he focuses on Christian initiation as entry into the paschal mystery. It is not just that the death and resurrection of Jesus two millennia ago is the sourcing power of our salvation and a paradigm human experience that provides the only ultimate intelligibility for our human condition, an understanding that we hope to transmit to each succeeding generation through appropriate catechesis and ritual celebration. Nor is it most basically the insight that the new life of risen existence which we hope to share with the glorified Christ necessarily grows out of self-giving love willing to go even to death for one's friends.

It is the risen Christ himself who is the paschal mystery; he is our pasch and as such is our hope. We are meant to share the full Spirit-life he now enjoys precisely in the way we share the spirit-life of others in that experience we call friendship; and sharing Christ's risen Spirit-life is meant to begin already in this life through our faith relationship to him.

Which leads us to the role of Christ's Spirit in the sacrament of confirmation, a role consistently mentioned but seldom explained in catechesis about the sacrament. Fourez's essay is a happy exception to the all too common vagueness about the conferring of the Spirit in confirmation. Much of the value of his explanation is his retention of a *functional* context of reflection; for him Christ's Spirit is not some abstract "third person of the Blessed Trinity" but rather a dynamic animating force at work personally in the consciousness of Christians.

What I think might be added to Fourez's already rich presentation is a greater emphasis on the *community* character of Christ's Spirit. Standard catechesis about "reception of the Holy Spirit" in initiation rituals has all too often created the impression of "the Spirit" being given from above to each individual. What the symbolic reality of the baptismal and confirmational liturgies conveys, however, is a different view: the new or renewed Christian comes to possession of Christ's Spirit precisely by sharing in this Spirit as possessed by the community. In the sacramental ritual the community is communicating to the person a greater share in the Spirit of the risen Lord by which it lives as a community of faith. And as Fourez very correctly points out, the animating power of Christ's Spirit in the "new" Christians enriches and expands the community's life in this Spirit.

Though he does not have space to develop the idea, Fourez opens up an important pastoral dimension of the confirmational catechesis, namely the way in which it can serve to overcome the generation gap that afflicts so many Christian groups. However, as he argues, it can do this only to the extent that the adults in a particular parish situation recognize, honor and listen to the working of Christ's Spirit in a younger generation. From the viewpoint of pedagogical theory this resonates strongly with Paulo Friere's insistence of the need to break with the "banking" approach to education.

Again to draw attention to something already prominent in one of the essays: Gary Davis' stress on religious experience—or, as he terms it a number of times, "spirituality"—as a prerequisite to theology. This sequence of experience and then explanation is, of course, honored in the great patristic mystagogical catecheses. But it is only common sense if one keeps sacramental catechesis in the context of personal relationship of people to God and to one another. There can be no meaningful explanation of an experience if there has been no meaningful experience; all there can be is an abstract academic lesson.

Three dimensions of Christian experience are essential; indeed, they are inseparable. There must be a growing experience of oneself as Christian; there must be a growing experience of the parish (or comparable group) as a Christian community; and there must be an experience of what these first two sacramentalize, namely God being revealed in the risen Christ and their Spirit. Preparation for the ritual of confirmation must be careful not to neglect any of the three.

Finally, to the question of the appropriate age for the ritual of confirmation. It seems to me that the essays in this volume make it unmistakably clear that there is little more that can be said as a contribution to the debate. Both those who insist that confirmation should be situated between baptism and first full participation in eucharist and those who wish to situate it sometime in adolescence are right, for the simple reason that there are two logics at work in the discussion. Liturgical logic points to the continued ritual linkage of confirmation with baptism; pastoral logic points to the psychological need for young people to publicly commit themselves in freedom to adult Christian life. This would seem to lead to an impasse with regard to actual practice, but I think that a way out of the impasse is suggested by Craig Cox's "not so modest proposal."

Recognizing the pastoral evidence—which all of the authors

seem to accept in one way or another—that at several stages of a Christian's development toward mature faith there is need for reaffirming the free decision to be Christian, Cox makes the sensible suggestion that there be an appropriate liturgy at each of these "passages." The first of these liturgies, which may well occur about the age of seven to ten and which signals the person's ability to participate personally and fully in eucharist, could be termed "confirmation" and be dealt with as the ritual fulfillment of the baptismal liturgy. In this way the logic of Christian ritual and historical tradition would be honored. Later liturgies that celebrated other moments in the lifelong process of initiation into the mystery of Christ could be named otherwise and might most effectively be celebrated in conjunction with focal eucharistic celebrations such as the Easter vigil. Arthur Kubick's essay suggests ways in which this ongoing "confirmation" could be integrated into the liturgical life of a parish. Indeed, a ritual of last anointing and viaticum could logically be celebrated as the last of these liturgies of "passage."

The fact that these later liturgies did not technically qualify for the name "the sacrament of confirmation" would not diminish their grace-giving effectiveness. Indeed, if the individual involved in the liturgy were better prepared than at an earlier age to commit himself or herself to the Christian lifestyle and to active discipleship, that person would share more fully in the Spirit that animates the church. John Westerhoff's insistence on the level of maturity required for free faith options reinforces this idea.

If one wished to reconcile this theological view within classical sacramental theology one could do so by employing the notion of *ex opere operantis*. It seems to me that resolution of the liturgico/theological debate about the confirmational liturgy's *temporal* relation to baptism is of secondary importance when compared with deciding what most leads people to deeper participation in the church's life and closer personal friendship with the risen Lord.

If such a "not so modest proposal" were to be accepted, it seems to me that all the insights of the authors of this volume, even those that seem to differ, could be affirmed. More importantly, the time and energy spent now on arguing for one or other age as that ideal for confirmation could be focused on celebrating more effectively the mystery of Christians' ongoing initiation into the life of Christ's Spirit.

CONTRIBUTORS

BERNARD COOKE is a sacramental theologian who teaches at Holy Cross College in Worcester, Massachusetts. Former president of the Catholic Theological Society of America, he has authored fourteen books including *Sacraments and Sacramentality* (Twenty-Third Publications).

CRAIG COX received a D.Min. from St. Mary's Seminary and University, Baltimore, in 1986. He studied canon law at Catholic University where he received the J.C.L. in 1987 and the J.C.D. in 1989. He serves on the Archdiocesan Tribunal in Los Angeles and is a member of the Archdiocesan Theological Commission there.

GARY DAVIS is pastor of Lake Oswego United Church of Christ in Lake Oswego, Oregon.

GÉRARD FOUREZ, S.J. teaches on the faculty of Notre Dame de la Paix in Namur, Belgium. He is the author of *Sacraments and Passages: Celebrating the Tensions of Modern Life* (Ave Maria Press).

THOMAS MARSH is professor of dogmatic theology at St. Patrick's College, Maynooth, Ireland. His articles have appeared in various scholarly journals, especially *The Irish Theological Quarterly* and *The Furrow*. His book, *Gift of Community: Baptism and Confirmation,* is part of the Message of the Sacraments series published by Michael Glazier, Inc.

ARTHUR J. KUBICK is director of religious education for St. Elizabeth of Hungary Church, Acton, Massachusetts. He is a member of the adjunct faculty of Boston College in the institute of religious education and pastoral ministry, and a consultant for *Professional Approaches for Christian Educators (PACE)* (Our Sunday Visitor).

LYNN NEU works as director of youth ministry for the archdiocese of Milwaukee.

RICHARD REICHERT is a consultant for adult and youth catechesis for the diocese of Green Bay, Wisconsin. He is an author for Brown Publishing-ROA Media for whom he has written a confirmation program for both junior and senior high youth.

KIERAN SAWYER, S.S.N.D. is a national authority on adolescent catechesis and is director of the TYME OUT Retreat Center in Milwaukee. She is an author for Ave Maria Press; among her publications is the popular *Confirming Faith*.

THERESA VIRAMONTES-GUTIERREZ is the Spanish-speaking consultant for the high school confirmation process for the Los Angeles archdiocese. She is also a member of the Los Angeles Office of Religious Education—Confirmation Task Force.

JOHN H. WESTERHOFF is an Episcopal priest in the diocese of North Carolina and professor of theology and Christian nurture at the Duke University Divinity School. His many books and articles include *Will Our Children Have Faith?* (Seabury) and *The Sacraments and the Cycle of Life* (Seabury).